THE STRANGLEHOLD

How to Break the Palestinians' Unyielding Grip
on the Middle East Peace Process

by Curtis Pontz

DORRANCE
PUBLISHING CO
EST. 1920
PITTSBURGH, PENNSYLVANIA 15238

Dorrance Publishing Co
585 Alpha Drive
Suite 103
Pittsburgh, PA 15238
Visit our website at www.dorrancebookstore.com

ISBN: 978-1-6366-1480-9
eISBN: 978-1-6366-1661-2

To my wife Leslie, my children Eden, Evan (of blessed memory), Ari, Jared, and Zach, and my grandchildren Alyssa, Aviva, Ethan, Fletcher, Jadan, Mya, Tahlia, and Zeke.

CONTENTS

"Israel was not created in order to disappear — Israel will endure and flourish. It is the child of hope and home of the brave. It can neither be broken by adversity nor demoralized by success. It carries the shield of democracy and it honors the sword of freedom."

-President John F. Kennedy, August 26th, 1960

"Make no mistake — those who adhere to the ideology of rejecting Israel's right to exist, they might as well reject the earth beneath them or the sky above, because Israel is not going anywhere."

-President Barack Obama, May 21st, 2015

PROLOGUE:

What You Need to Know

Let me be clear. I am Jewish. I have a great affection for Judaism. I am proud of my Jewish identity, and work overtime to strengthen that identity. And as is pertinent to this book's theme, I believe that those Jewish people who have wished to live together in a Jewish land should have always had, and must always have, the opportunity and absolute right to do so. Lastly, in the interest of making full disclosure in light of my steadfast connections to the Jewish faith, I admit that I love the fragrance of kosher salamis hanging from the ceilings of Jewish delicatessens.

My motive for setting out the above disclosures (the last of which may very well be irrelevant) is because this book bears directly on the creation of the modern State of Israel in 1948, and on the continuing objection of the Palestinians to Israel's presence in the Middle East, so I wanted to make it abundantly clear where my heart stands. However, notwithstanding that I take great pride in my Jewish faith and heritage, and that I tend to find myself in sync with Israel on geopolitical issues, the goal of this book is not to champion or advance any particular cause on behalf of Israel or Jewish people in the world today except to indirectly promote the fundamental tenet of safeguarding the continued existence of the State of Israel.

Nor is it my aim to voice opinions regarding any past or current political positions adopted by the government of Israel or contained in the pronouncements of elected or appointed Israeli public officials. I won't delve into various questions of a legal nature, such as whether the West Bank is occupied territory or disputed territory, or the legality of the West Bank settlements. Nor will this book discuss the present or past policies of Israel's government concerning the country's security needs or military objectives, or the placement of settlements in the West Bank, or Israel's policy of home demolitions of Palestinians charged with killing Israelis, or Israel's blockade of Gaza designed to restrict the entry into Gaza of weapons and of construction materials for repurposing to build tunnels leading from Gaza into Israel. This book won't deal with the Boycott, Divestment, and Sanctions (BDS) movement that looks to wreak economic havoc on Israel and arguably seeks Israel's destruction. And I have no intent to contemplate in any respect the possible terms and conditions of any prospective peace agreement between Israel and the Palestinians. Without going on, you hopefully grasp the scope of subjects that this book is not meant to cover.

Instead, what I will address in this book is solely the narrow but impactful topic of whether the State of Israel, embedded where it now sits in the Middle East, was justifiably and justly created. More precisely, I will address whether Israel was justifiably and justly created as the place to which the Jewish people were able to return to establish and perpetuate a Jewish state. This, after the Jewish people had been driven all over the world during 1,900 years of exile following the destruction of Jerusalem and the Second Temple by the Romans in 70 C.E.

There is a distinct reason I target this precise issue. That reason pertains to, and flows from, the critical linkage that I firmly believe exists between the fact of Israel being located in the Middle East and the inability, indeed the miserable failure of everyone concerned, to resolve the so-called Israel-Palestinian conflict. More exactly, I believe the very fact of Israel's position on the map of the Middle East is what has served as the impetus for the rejection by the Palestinians of the seemingly countless efforts towards conflict resolution. Parenthetically, although Israel is more accurately cited as being located in the Near East, I will refer to the Middle East rather than to the Near East to reduce the risk that any reader will become geographically disoriented.

I have long been frustrated beyond measure by the continuing efforts, pursued by those involved in the peace-making process, to formulate a path to peace between Israel and the Palestinians without realistically taking into account the underlying obstacle to reaching some meaningful accommodation (something less than an agreement to love one another would do just fine) between the two parties. What is that obstacle? It is the well-documented historical refusal of the Palestinians to accept the legitimacy and existence of a sovereign Jewish state at the spot in the Middle East where that nation was established in 1948. My bottom line premise is that unless or until the Palestinians accept the legitimacy and existence of the sovereign State of Israel exactly where Israel now sits on the world map, there can be no practical path to a negotiated peace between the two sides. Other writers have opined the same premise using a variety of phrasing, but invariably as only a portion of a commentary covering many different aspects of the Israel-Palestinian conflict. This book does not veer from its narrow focus of concern.

In an ideal world, those interested in formulating a route to peace would have engaged in a string of spirited international conversations about the real obstacle to a negotiated peace between Israel and the Palestinians. They would have discussed the unwillingness of the Palestinians to accept the legitimacy and existence of Israel. They would have pressed to break the stranglehold that this Palestinian stance has had upon the peace process. However, for reasons not relevant to this book, but which are no doubt tied to a tendency to shy away from requiring the Palestinians to accept responsibility or accountability for the Israel-Palestinian conflict, conversations about the above-stated obstacle have invariably been sidetracked or circumvented. So my frustration over the failure of past proponents of peace to confront or acknowledge what is at the core of the conflict had grown to the point where it made sense to me that if I expected my frustration to be heard and understood,

I had better convey my thoughts to the attention of a broader audience than that with which I would typically engage in social conversation. I needed to satisfy my urge to open up a candid discussion of the topic with a wide range of people.

It is quite important to me that I do my part to help generate a dialogue about the real obstacle to peace. Why? The explanation lies in my belief that the Palestinians' resistance to the acceptance of the presence of Israel in its present location must be crushed, because only by doing so can it be reasonably anticipated that a pathway to a negotiated peace can be realized. I find appealing the thought of an end to the impasse between Israel and the Palestinians. It spells a future where Israel will be able to live in enduring peace with its neighbors. Thus I undertook this book, which is directed to the attention of people of all backgrounds and political persuasions.

But at the same time as I became driven to write to express my thoughts, I sensed that I ought to tread carefully in my writing. First, I felt the need to be respectful of the obvious truth that no one has all the answers required to resolve the conflict (although I hasten to note that my understanding of the matters to which the subsequent chapters of this book refer has deepened over the years). Second, I am acutely aware that other people may not see the world as I do. Third, I do not want to risk unnecessarily distracting the reader's focus from this book's theme by injecting or incorporating other issues, such as those cited in the third paragraph of this Prologue. So I battled with my inner-self to write a book that does not cloud any more than is necessary the explicit task at hand, namely trying to meet the formidable challenge of persuading the Palestinians to accept the legitimacy and existence of the sovereign Jewish State of Israel by convincing them that its creation was justifiable and just (and if I cannot convince the Palestinians, a goal that may be beyond my reach, maybe I can at least convince some of those who are in a position to convince the Palestinians). I believe, as I will repeatedly assert, that the key to overcoming the Palestinians' long-standing rejection of the presence in the Middle East of a sovereign Jewish state is to successfully make the argument that the establishment of Israel was justifiable and just.

Again to assure that the reader does not get sidetracked by peripheral issues, my writing at no point is intended to personally denigrate those who apply what I or others might consider being double standards or biases that could be viewed as an attempt to undermine the legitimacy and existence of the State of Israel. And I have tried my best to recite objectively my understanding of historical outcomes rather than through a Jewish lens, although that may have been easier said than done. After all, many fair-minded observers, both Jewish and non-Jewish, have long been convinced by events that the concept of recognizing Israel's legitimacy and right to exist is seen by the Palestinians (and Arab Muslims in general) as tantamount to accepting the presence of Jews on land the Palestinians believe belongs solely to the Islamic and Arab worlds. This, of course, has been the basis for the Palestinians' rejection of the legitimacy and right to exist of the sovereign State of Israel. And those same fair-minded observers may very well perceive that the Palestinians have not ever been willing to broker a compromise in connection with their denial of Israel's legitimacy and right to exist. But even in the face of these seeming roadblocks to making any headway in persuading the Palestinians to accept Israel as their neighbor, I have tried to be objective in my writing.

In my view, there is no realistic likelihood that anyone can negotiate a peace accord if the Palestinians do not first accept the creation and continuing presence amidst the Arab world of the Jewish State of Israel. So this book will attempt to lay out the pertinent facts in support of the conclusion Israel's establishment was warranted, i.e., was justifiable and just. To me, there seems no other way to transform the Palestinians' line of reasoning, upon which their unwillingness to accept Israel's legitimacy and existence is based, except by stoking the fires of passionate debate.

I am not suggesting that the Palestinians' century-long rejection, first of the concept and then of the creation of the Jewish State of Israel, is the only problem preventing a solution to the conflict. For example, it will be difficult under any set of circumstances to move full speed ahead with a peace process if acts of terrorism do not wane, or if both sides do not bring moderates to the negotiating table. However, it appears clear that the door to a workable peace deal will remain stuck in the closed position until the Palestinians work through their refusal to accept Israel's presence in their neighborhood. For those who predict that the polarizing discourse between the Palestinians and Israelis will never cease and that the conflict will never end, I regrettably suggest a fulfilled prophecy so long as the obstacle to peace I cite remains in play.

There have been numerous theories and rationales for why the State of Israel should, or should not, have been established in its Middle East locale. Some of those arguments have been debunked as silly or vapid. Others have gained a major level of acceptance in the Arab world and beyond. In any case, both sides' arguments will hopefully be touched upon with a high degree of even-handedness throughout. Given my admittedly pro-Israel sensitivities, that has not been an easy challenge. However, due to my lack of personal ties to Israel and my interest in cultivating an environment in which the reader can feel confident that a major objective of this book is to produce a productive outcome, I am optimistic that I will succeed in convincing readers that my only allegiance is to being fair-minded.

But it is one thing to try, by relating the author's honorable intentions, to create the impression that an author is fair-minded and even-handed. It is another thing to present the evidence in that way. Readers can best make a decision or draw a conclusion if they have been sufficiently and accurately informed about the subject at hand. As is valid with all the issues surrounding the complex Israel-Palestinian conflict, people have become divided along typically partisan battle lines, with the not unsurprising result that the struggle to engage in a fruitful discussion becomes impeded. The disagreement typically hastens more confrontation and worsens because it is difficult to resolve differences with people who may have a different worldview. So it is vital that those debating the issues are adequately informed. In this vein and context, I have attempted to offer a method for laying out the script to which those paying attention to developments in the Middle East may not be accustomed. I do not view my task in writing this book as merely setting forth a chronicle of events. My technique involves presenting the pros and cons upon which the question of the justification and justness of Israel's founding can be considered and evaluated. Using this approach, I hope to enable the reader to effectively draw a conclusion to that question by balancing the points in favor versus the points against.

Thus, I contemplate that the question of whether Israel was justifiably and justly created (which, if resolved in the affirmative, offers the promise of laying to rest the Palestinian objection to the legitimacy and continued existence of the State of Israel) will be decided by the reader on the weight of all the evidence, and not based on any one particular argument or point. It is better that the pros and cons are considered as part of a total package. The stronger arguments then are weighted in favor of either the positive or negative position, rather than a single isolated pro or con being allowed to dictate one's conclusion. After all, a particular pro or con may be nothing more than a stale talking point, or based on a spin of the facts, or driven by the reputation of the source of information, or be outweighed by the preponderance of sound contrary considerations. On the other hand, deciding a question based on the weight of all the available and pertinent evidence promises to lead to a more thoughtful, logical, and supportable conclusion.

Please understand that I am not attempting to twist anyone's arm to gain agreement that Israel's presence in the Middle East is both justifiable and just. To the contrary, I leave it to you, the reader, to draw a conclusion based on your weighing the evidence upon which this book elaborates. You will be the judge of how persuasive the evidence is one way or the other. But I stress that I do not hesitate to lay out the facts even when they fly in the face of the Palestinian perspective. In addition, where I feel the evidence presented deserves an expression of my agreement or disagreement or approval or disapproval, I will offer opinion. In doing so, I am not attempting to orchestrate your thought process. But I do recognize that my personal sentiments could be colored by emotion. Even so, I do not believe that the expression of my personal beliefs has in any instance influenced how I present the underlying factual information or evidence.

Note that there are no footnotes. I want the reader to view the book's premise and its presentation as coming from the heart and not as scholarly literature. I have no interest in trying to establish myself as a researcher. Also, footnotes have not been included out of concern that the identity of the source of a particular point will be seized upon as the sole element of proof of the correctness of the conclusion as to whether the establishment of Israel in the land of Palestine was justifiable and just. I want the conclusion to be based on the weight of all the evidence bearing on the question of whether Jews are entitled to dwell in a sovereign Jewish state comprising land to which the Palestinians claim sole entitlement. I am confident that anyone who wishes to question any evidentiary matter to which reference is made will be able, notwithstanding the absence of footnotes identifying information sources, to quickly conduct research aimed at unearthing contrary information. I am furthermore convinced my commentary's factual accuracy will stand up to any challenge.

I must add and emphasize that the release in late January 2020 of President Donald Trump's peace plan, the so-called "deal of the century," has no impact on the content of this book except in one respect — that being the reaction of the Palestinian Arabs to the plan. On one hand, the Arab world generally responded to the proposal either with restraint or silence. Several Arab governments even hinted that the plan was welcomed, if ever so cautiously, as a basis for negotiations (apparently it is no longer a certainty that the Arab countries will always fall in line with the Palestinians in denying and decrying the existence of Israel – perhaps this is because most of the Arab states now have far more pressing concerns than the fate of the Palestinians).

On the other hand, the Palestinians rejected the Trump plan out-of-hand, not only when the plan was released but also before its issuance when its provisions were still unknown. I could perhaps be convinced that the dislike that the Palestinians feel for President Trump due to his apparent pro-Israel positions would have served as legitimate grounds for rejecting the plan once its content became public. However, I would be swayed in that direction only if someone could satisfactorily explain to me why the Palestinians have rejected, over and over, peace overtures and plans put forward by prior U.S. administrations. But to disavow the not-yet-released proposal without even knowing what it contained reinforces, at least in my judgment, the long-standing pattern of Palestinian rejection of Israel's legitimacy and right to exist.

So while it appears that some Arab rulers (if not the bulk of the Arab citizenry) are coming to terms with the reality of Israel's legitimacy and existence, the Palestinian response to the Trump plan signals that nothing has changed concerning the unwillingness of the Palestinians to accept the presence in the Middle East of the Jewish State of Israel. Consequently, we again face the dilemma of how peace can be forged between Israel and the Palestinians if the Palestinians continue to refuse to accept, as seemingly reflected most recently in their outright rejection of the "deal of the century," the legitimacy and existence of a sovereign Jewish state where it is situated in the Middle East? As I have maintained, the place to start is to convince the Palestinians that Israel's creation was both justifiable and just.

As you delve into the portion of this book that discusses the pros and cons bearing upon the question of whether Israel's establishment was justifiable and just, hopefully you will determine, based on the weight of the evidence presented, that Israel's creation was precisely that, i.e., both justifiable and just. If you reach that conclusion, then you will hopefully join me in conveying the message to the peacemakers, and others with a need to know, that it is time to stop ignoring, underestimating, circumventing, or glossing over discussion of the depth of the resistance of the Palestinians to the legitimacy and existence of Israel. Let us all realize that a negotiated peace will not be achieved until that key impediment, or what I have referred to as the real obstacle to resolving the Israel-Palestinian conflict, is overcome. The world cannot continue to close its eyes, or its minds, to the fact that the core issue for the Palestinians remains the continued existence of Jewish sovereignty in the Middle East. I am convinced that once that core obstacle to peace is overcome, a negotiated resolution of the Israel-Palestinian conflict is possible.

You may ask, who am I to think that my thoughts have merit or even deserve reflection on the matter of ending a conflict that has raged for over 100 years, and in connection with which hundreds of brilliant minds have floundered in seeking a solution to the impasse between the two parties? After all, I am not an academic, historian, intellectual, politician, diplomat, or otherwise blessed with a background that might provide me an edge over other pundits. Well, the short answer is that this book is written by someone who has strived to become well-informed on the subject, who wants to see the ugly conflict resolved fairly, and who has made an effort to present information objectively, both in the form of facts and opinion, aimed at moving forward the process of finding a peaceful solution. Hopefully, my words will stir others' interest in joining with me in whatever role one chooses to assume in attempting to forge positive movement towards an enduring peace.

For clarity, I want to define my use of the term "Palestinians." In this discussion, "Palestinians" are those Arab people now living in Palestine (composed of modern-day Israel, the West Bank, and Gaza), or who once lived there but left at any time after November 29, 1947 (the day the United Nations approved its partition plan) and now live as refugees in Arab lands.

And I also want to explain that I hold out little hope that those who engage in schemes to target Israel's extinction will be swayed by what I have to say. Accordingly, this book targets two other distinct groups. The first is that cohort of people who are already motivated, or are ripe to be motivated, to attempt to convince the Palestinians or those who may be able to convince the Palestinians, that it is time for the Palestinians to abandon their rejection of Israel's legitimacy and right to exist. Second, I am also aiming for that broad swath of people who are supportive of the Palestinian "cause." People anywhere are entitled to express solidarity with the Palestinian "cause," or to assert their views about Israel. Still, such solidarity or views should not be allowed to stand if uninformed, misinformed, or the result of disregarding important facts. I include in the group of critics of Israel and supporters of the Palestinian "cause" those who (a) think they know what is best for Israel without having much historical awareness, (b) expect Israel to resolve the conflict because of the military and economic power it wields, (c) buy into the Palestinian view of history because they have heard it so often that they figure it must be true, (d) follow flawed assumptions that, for whatever reasons, they are not up to the challenge of reassessing, a good example of a flawed assumption being that a peace accord has not been reached because Israel is not interested in achieving peace, and/or (e) perceive the Palestinians as the underdog (and who doesn't like the underdog?). I am looking to the possibility that those who fall into the above categories will be influenced by my words to reconsider their pro-Palestinian (or anti-Israel) position by carefully weighing whether Israel's establishment was justifiable and just. By coming down on the side of those who argue that Israel's creation was justifiable and just, you remove yourself from among those who are offering encouragement to the Palestinians unwilling to accept Israel's legitimacy and right to exist.

One last comment is in order before you begin considering and weighing the evidence related to determining whether the establishment of Israel was justifiable and just. Throughout this book, I continually refer to "the Palestinians" as though the Palestinians are of one mind in rejecting Israel's legitimacy and existence and wanting to erase it from the map of the Middle East. However, I fully recognize that not all Palestinians were in the past or are presently unwilling to accept the presence of Israel in the Middle East. I will take that comment one step further and acknowledge that there are members of the Palestinian community who are hopeful that peace with Israel can someday be achieved. Some Palestinians, certainly more than a few among those who have managed to reject anti-Israel indoctrination and propaganda, are undoubtedly even eager to arrive at a peaceful solution to the conflict. But sadly, one cannot ignore that all too often, Palestinians who believe in promoting dialogue with Israelis are silenced or effectively deterred from doing so by Palestinian ideologues who insist that there be no defections from the rejectionist front or who threaten reprisals.

For a Palestinian to even suggest accepting Israel's legitimacy and existence will typically lead to severe rebuke or worse. A Palestinian who, in any manner, recognizes Israel's legitimacy and right to exist is likely to be viewed by fellow Palestinians as having committed an act of treason. Palestinians who attempt to promote economic cooperation between the two sides are condemned by other Palestinians for engaging in treacherous activity. Those whom I consider to be the well-intentioned Palestinians ultimately have no influence on the behavior of those Arabs who harbor a jihadist mentality. It seems as though the Palestinians who wish the peace process to move forward are always "overpowered" by the rejectionists. Of course, there is also the significant impact of the radical Islamists on the Palestinian psyche, a subject that is way beyond this book's scope. In light of the difficulties encountered by the moderate Palestinians in gaining a toehold on Palestinian public opinion, I must proceed on the basis that it is the most outspoken Palestinian voices that hold sway, and that it is those persons who must be persuaded to change course. It is, therefore, to those who dictate and control the Palestinian position of rejection of Israel's legitimacy and right to exist that I am referring when I cite "the Palestinians."

CHAPTER 1:

The Zionist Movement - A Look Back

There have been so many crises in the life of the Jewish people that anyone keeping tabs probably lost count long ago. But history reveals that the Jewish people never succumbed. They always have, or so it seems in the final analysis, been persistent in exhibiting the will to live. They have adapted as best they could to new circumstances, even when others ripped their former community ties apart. They typically did all they could to maintain a Jewish environment for themselves, despite the depletion of their spiritual energy as they struggled to adjust to new local cultures into which they were thrown. However, during the latter decades of the 19th century, many Jews began observing what they believed to be initial signs of the decadence of Jewish religious life throughout the world, and they foresaw the possible demise in the long-term of Jewish religious practice and even the death of Jewish culture. But of more immediate concern to these Jews was their sense that the Jewish people's traditions were slipping away from a large portion of the world's

Jewish population due to the forces of assimilation. The threat of assimilation was perceived to be ominous, particularly in Western Europe and in the United States.

Along with the pressing worry about the likely future acceleration in the rate of assimilation, there was an increasing fear that for those Jews who persevered in holding onto their Jewish roots and practices, the prejudice felt by non-Jews against the Jewish people as a continually diminishing minority group would increase in intensity. After all, the dilemma for any dispersed minority group is that it has no center where the opposition to the prejudice can efficiently organize and from where the resistance can draw its strength. So what was to be done to stem the tide of events, resulting from the impact of assimilation and its consequences, that appeared to be threatening the preservation of Jewish traditions? What was to be done about the growing sense among Jews who were invested in their faith that the Jewish people's dissolution was, if not just around the corner, at least posing as a future possibility? What was to be done to reconstruct the bonds among Jews that had existed during all of Jewish post-biblical history, but were now thought to be withering away?

In simplistic terms, it was a question of group survival. How was Jewish life going to be perpetuated? How could world Jewry ward off the danger of disintegration? How could it effectively confront the seeming threat to its very existence? Yes, the Jewish people had proven over 3,000 years that they had the will to live. But in the face of accelerating assimilation, the prospects for the survival of Jewry looked increasingly bleak. Those struggling with the predicament were trying to uncover and define the key to preventing the collapse of the world of Jewry. What was to be the solution? How radical of a fix was required? If the Jewish people easily understood anything, it was that the fundamental underpinning of survival is self-preservation. Among those for whom Judaism was a matter of devotion and who cringed thinking of eventual dissolution, some were frightened into despair. But others were spurred into action. If the process of decay of the Jewish people was ongoing and inevitable, then those who were most concerned with the approaching dissolution felt extreme steps had to be taken to prevent the ultimate disappearance of Judaism. Coincidently, and no doubt of potential impact, was the fact that lurking in the background was the concept of the land of Palestine serving as home to the Jewish people and as the center of Jewish life in the world. This refrain had been constant throughout Jewish history.

What evolved out of this fear for the Jewish people's fate was something called Zionism, alternatively referred to as the Zionist movement, and often defined as the national liberation movement of the Jewish people. The name "Zionism" comes from the word "Zion," a Hebrew term that refers to Jerusalem. Zionism was formally devised at the first International Zionist Conference in 1897 as a movement aimed at securing for Jews a safe home in Palestine, considered by Jews as being the ancestral home of the Jewish people, for those Jews not wanting to remain where they were then living. The inspiration for Zionism was Theodore Herzl, a Hungarian

the University of Vienna. A journalist by profes-
~as a secular Jew.

Individual Jews migrated to Palestine every century since the destruction of Jerusalem and the Second Temple by the Romans in 70 C.E. There had been occasional references in 19th century literature to the notion of advocating for the restoration of normal community life for the Jewish people centered in Palestine, especially following the devastating effect of massacres of Jews in Russia in 1887. But the Zionist movement did not begin to generate momentum until the first decade of the 20th century. It would not be overstating the case to cite the Zionist movement as being in the vanguard of the effort to assure the Jewish people's survival regardless of where on earth they then lived. More succinctly, Zionism aimed to obtain a safe home in Palestine for the Jewish people. The idea was that the existence of that home would be secured by international laws or guarantees, the exact nature or construct of which had not yet been formulated by anyone linked to the Zionist movement. Zionism stood for the proposition that the Jews would no longer stake their future as a dispersed people on their ability to survive without the benefits of a center for Jewish life in Palestine.

An offshoot of the Zionist movement's primary goal was to positively impact those Jews who would not be returning to Palestine, but who would remain scattered throughout the world in the Diaspora (the places where dispersed Jews settled) and presumably continue to succumb to hostile social forces that inevitably lead to the disintegration of minorities. The thinking

The idea of Jewish nationality, was added at this time

went that the prospect of a fulfilling life in Palestine for a significant number of Jewish people could provide an impetus for those Jews who were to remain dispersed in the Diaspora to continue to maintain their identity as Jews. It was anticipated that Zionism would have meaning not just to the Jews who would eagerly move to Palestine, but also to Jews remaining in the Diaspora. They would become reinvigorated and joyously claim identity with the source of their new-found pride. Of course, the effort to preserve the Jews who would remain in the Diaspora was not incompatible with the undertaking to encourage Jews scattered about the world to migrate to Palestine.

It is essential to keep in mind that it was not the Zionist movement's goal to relocate the entire population of world Jewry in Palestine. Nor was the intention to segregate all the Jews in the world in Palestine. Instead, the aim was to preserve the Jewish people. And what more logical place for the survival effort to be launched than in Palestine? It was the historic home of the Jewish people. (Without going into any detail, know that the British at one time or another had offered the Sinai Peninsula and later Uganda as the site of a Jewish homeland). Even though the Zionists were pushing a plan to perpetuate the existence of the Jewish people, their movement promoted the concept of the return to Palestine of only some share of the worldwide Jewish population. It was understood that Palestine would become a home for Jews who were going to migrate there, but that many Jews, for a variety of reasons, would not gravitate towards Palestine. As Herzl stated in 1898, no one among the Zionists expected that all Jews would go to Palestine.

It was assumed many Jews would continue to live as Jews in the Diaspora and would have no objection to the Zionist movement, but that they would not join or support the effort to concentrate in Palestine those Jews who wanted to establish an environment in the land of their ancestors, where Jewish life could be renewed and a common heritage preserved.

Let's change gears for a moment and again ask some questions. What was the evil in Jews rallying behind a movement founded upon recognition and realization that the survival of the Jewish people had long been dependent upon a struggle to maintain faith in spiritual-based traditions? What was the evil in preserving the institutions and traditions representing what the Zionists considered the heart and soul of the Jewish people? What was the evil in seeking to establish the geographical unity of the Jewish people? After century upon century marked by inquisitions, expulsions, pogroms, and massacres of Jews in countries to which the Jewish people had been dispersed, what was the evil in attempting to accomplish these objectives by constructing a plan of rejuvenation in the land of Palestine, the home of their forefathers? This latter question is at the heart of the matter that this book addresses.

It is, of course, true that there were Jews, to whom I will further refer shortly, who rejected or distorted the hope of the Jews who wished for Palestine to once again serve as the center of Jewish life in the world. But that circumstance did not really matter to the Zionists. The Jews who did not foresee or anticipate the possible extinction of Judaism were, in the minds of those engaged in the Zionist movement, likely doomed to be assimilated into the non-Jewish world. It was more critical to focus on the Jews who desired to live and hopefully thrive as a rejuvenated group bound by common ties based on traditions. According to the Zionist movement, that aspiration could best be expressed in the undertaking to rebuild and strengthen Jewish life in Palestine. Not wanting to see the Jews devoured by the forces of assimilation, the Zionists were determined to prove that only in their historic land, where the Jews could safely affirm their culture, could a Jewish way of life be sustained. The Zionist movement believed that the Jewish people had no other avenue of escape from their slide into oblivion than to reestablish a home and center of Jewish life in Palestine. Zionism was pushing the theme that the Jews had better not stake their future well-being on the expectation that they could survive as a dispersed people without a center where everyday Jewish life could and would flourish.

What kind of people were those Jews who were at the forefront of a project that they anticipated would lead to the reconstruction of a homeland for the world's Jews in their ancient homeland? It was no doubt true that virtually every participant in the Zionist movement was passionate about their endeavor. They were willing to sacrifice to ideals in whatever ways became necessary as they toiled in the land of their ancestors. Though virtually all of the pioneers were Jewish, some had little or no interest in practicing their faith, and a few doubted or even denied that a God existed. The major portion of the newcomers were socialists, a segment were communists, and not so many were capitalists. But whatever their economic system preference, the Zionists who arrived in Palestine were imbued with physical courage and stamina of the sort required to meet the challenges they were facing. They were artisans, farmers, peddlers, merchants, teachers, musicians, construction workers, etc., almost all people of extremely modest means. Few of them were prompted to settle in Palestine by the prospect of personal gain or profit, but rather by the allure of ideals to which they were devoted related to the history of the Jewish people. Although there were no economic pulls in the early stages of the migration, as time passed, the draw of economic opportunity became more compelling to some of the Zionists who moved to Palestine. But as a general proposition, what motivated the Zionist pioneers was the opportunity to live in a setting where freedom existed for the Jewish people, particularly where life could play out without being obstructed by violence or impacted by social stigma.

While individual Jews had been migrating to Palestine in scattered numbers over the many centuries of dispersion commencing in 70 C.E., it was not until the early 1880's that Jews began a migration involving a steady flow of people to Palestine, then a sparsely inhabited province that was part of the Ottoman Empire. The land in the portion of Palestine that became Israel was variously described by historians and demographers before the arrival of Jews at the beginning of the 1880's as thinly populated, unoccupied, uninhabited, and almost abandoned. That the land of Palestine to which the Jews started returning in the 1880's was barren and forlorn was underscored by author Mark

Twain's description of what he observed when he visited Palestine in 1867:

> [Palestine is a] desolate country whose soil is rich enough, but is given over wholly to weeds - a silent mournful expanse ... A desolation is here that not even imagination can grace with the pomp of life and action ... We never saw a human being on the whole route ... There was hardly a tree or shrub anywhere. Even the olive and the cactus, those fast friends of the worthless soil, had almost deserted the country.

Yet the record of what those settlers accomplished starting in the 1880's is both well-preserved and extraordinary. They drained the swamps and marshes that crisscrossed the then barren and desolate Palestinian landscape, quashing the hoards of mosquitoes and resultant malaria, and the deserts became blooming spectacles. They constructed canals, and created lush fields containing vineyards, orange groves, and almond and olive trees. They cultivated many different fruits, vegetables, and flora. They planted forests and forested rocky hillsides. They introduced scientific farming methods and modern farming machinery. Industries related to agriculture were established, and eventually rapid progress occurred in the broader industrial sector. The functions of government were developed. So, for example, public hygiene and sanitation, the water supply, and the streets and roads became the subject of government supervision and regulation. Policemen and tax assessors were employed. A completely diversified school system, including schools for agricultural studies and manual training, was developed. Museums of art and natural history were established, as were public libraries and hospitals serving people of all religious faiths. The press included daily newspapers and magazines on a variety of subjects. A university was founded. The ancient Hebrew language was revived. The Jewish men and women coming to the land of Palestine made short shrift of their project to bury forever in the graveyard of history the woes of the wandering Jew.

The pioneers' Palestinian Arab neighbors were mostly peasants working the land as tenants of wealthy Arabs from numerous countries who had purchased the land from those peasants (who had formerly owned the land and had been working it as what we would today call "small farmers") according to laws promulgated by the Ottoman Empire in the mid-nineteenth century. The Arab residents, although landless and working the land as tenants, nonetheless benefitted from the endeavors of the early Zionists in turning the land green. Arab farming methods progressed. The Arab villages prospered as the landscape transformed. The infant mortality rate among Palestinian Arabs plummeted. The life expectancy of the Palestinians grew by leaps and bounds, as did their literacy rate. It had to have appeared to the objective observer that Arab development in the form of an increased standard of living (by Western standards) accompanied the growth of the Jewish communities.

As for the treatment of the Arabs by the Zionists who had made Palestine their home, it is well-documented that the Jews established and supported Arab schools in which Arabs taught Arab children on various subjects, including the Koran. Arab workers found significant employment opportunities in the construction industry and in public works project operations. Health care for the Palestinians improved significantly. It might even be said that the relationship between the Arabs and Jews was harmonious — that the Palestinian Arab villagers had adapted to the peaceful environment in which they found themselves. After all, the Jews were living on land they had legally purchased, and were working the land with their bare hands and were living in stressed economic circumstances. So there was no apparent reason for the Arabs to fear that the Jews were intending in the future to claim some portion of Palestine as theirs. It is critical to emphasize that the efforts of the Zionists to build a presence in Palestine were marked by the purchase of the land, farms, and homes that were acquired. The Zionists did not steal any property to which they obtained title – it was all purchased by legal means. It is indisputable that there was no theft of property owned by Palestinians because there is no record anywhere of anyone complaining.

However, in the interest of not appearing to gloss over the subtle and not-so-subtle undercurrents of the period prior to 1920, it needs to be noted that there was some random resistance offered by the Palestinians even before 1920 to the Jewish immigration into Palestine. While there were occasional demonstrations by Palestinians, results of the efforts to incite the Palestinians against the Jews rarely rose to the level of anything approximating riots, and none of the protest gatherings resulted in the loss of life. It cannot be stated with certainty, but it does not appear the sentiment of the masses of Palestinians before 1920 reflected a fear or even concern that public or private interests of the Palestinian Arabs faced any danger as a result of the Jews' continuing immigration. Nor does there appear to be any record of the Zionist movement not being willing to accept the presence of Arabs in Palestine, or any attempt to expel or transfer anyone from the territory the Jews were cohabiting with the Palestinians. There is no reference to the idea of expelling Arabs from Palestine in any of Herzl's public writings, including political treatises, or any of his private correspondence or speeches. Even the militant faction within the Zionist movement declared in 1923 that no effort would ever be undertaken to eject anyone from Palestine. In a 1944 document titled "To Our Arab Neighbors," future Israeli Prime Minister Menachem Begin stated, "We do not see you as an enemy. We want to see you as good neighbors. We did not come to destroy you or expel you from the lands you live on...." In short, Zionism was never about replacing Arabs.

Due to a lack of preserved information on the subject, we can't recount in any meaningful detail what the Palestinians were thinking about the presence of the Zionist pioneers during the first few decades of the migration of Zionists to Palestine commencing at the very end of the 19th century. But there is some knowledge about the nature of the objections voiced by a relatively small minority of Jews to the Zionist movement. It might be instructive to discuss those opposing views. Initially, many of the Jews who disagreed with the Zionists did so because (a) they were obsessed with selfish fears that their status in their particular Jewish community would be diminished if Palestine became the world's center of Jewish life, (b) they mistook the aims of the movement, (c) they were fearful that Jewish minorities in the Diaspora would somehow suffer as a consequence of a Jewish home established in Palestine, and/or (d) they charged that Zionism was creating a perplexing dilemma for Jews in that they would face the issue of dual allegiance or dual loyalty between the land where they lived and the land of Palestine. None of those objections will be dealt with here because they do not bear upon possible consequences to the Palestinians.

There were, however, several specific objections raised by the Jewish anti-Zionists that arguably could be associated with the Palestinian viewpoint, and they must be considered. First, though the anti-Zionists generally conceded that the Jews once possessed the land on which they developed spiritually and that it had remained the spiritual home of world Jewry, they asserted that the Jews took possession of Palestine through conquest but then lost it to the Romans almost two thousand years ago by war. Thus the argument went that the Jews had no further claim to the land. But there is no historical precedent for the proposition that loss by conquest represents the relinquishment or abandonment of a territorial claim. History is replete with cases where seized land claims have been recognized because the descendants of the people who were expelled by force by an invader were living and asserted the claim.

However, the Jewish anti-Zionists would then further point out that since the Arabs also conquered Palestine, title to Palestinian land based on conquest applied to the Arabs as well as to the Jews, and that it was not possible to justify favoring the claim of the Jews over that of the Arabs. What was ignored in that line of thinking was that the Jews conquered Palestine to serve as their home. To the conquering Arabs, Palestine represented nothing more than a smidgen of sparsely settled land that became absorbed into a massive area in the Middle East and Africa that the Arabs possessed. Palestine was just one more piece of the earth's surface over which the Arab world gained control, and the proof "is in the pudding." Palestine never accrued any significant tangible or material benefit whatsoever, at least none of which the author was ever or has become aware, as a result of the Arab conquest of the land of Palestine and the people who lived there. Having just mentioned the issue of competing claims to the land, I will be returning in a later chapter to the fundamental factor that history reflects that both Jews and the Palestinians lay claim to the land of Palestine, and that if there is merit to the claim of each party, then compromise by both sides could have reasonably been anticipated to occur. But I am getting ahead of myself.

Also, the Jewish anti-Zionists expressed concern that once the migration of Jews to Palestine reached some magical level, the Jews could very well wish to recover various holy places and landmarks and thereby spur deadly religious confrontations, if not a full-blown religious war. But as we know, there have never been any confrontations connected with those holy sites

Israeli:
Military presence

in Israel that are linked to other faiths (except for intermittent disturbances tied to the Al-Aqsa Mosque in Jerusalem). As the Zionists made clear, the Jews did not have any interest then or in the future of assuming any responsibility for the non-Jewish holy places. Indeed, following the unification of Jerusalem during the 1967 Arab-Israel war, Israel handed over administrative control of the Temple Mount, considered the most sacred site in Judaism, to the Muslim Waqf. The Waqf, a Jordanian entity that had previously (prior to 1948) overseen the mosques built on the site, including the Al-Aqsa Mosque, retains the Temple Mount's custodianship to this day. Security has remained Israel's responsibility, and Israel has ultimate sovereignty over the Temple Mount. Inconceivably, at least in the eyes of a sizeable number of Jews, when Israel ceded administrative control of the Temple Mount to the Muslim Waqf, it gave up the basic Jewish right allowing Jews to pray at the Temple Mount. This signaled to the Palestinians that the sanctity of the Al-Aqsa Mosque would be protected and preserved, and the status quo has been maintained since 1967. The State of Israel is justifiably proud that it has always fully protected the holy sites located in Israel of all religions.

So that takes us to the argument advanced by the Jewish opponents of Zionism that, notwithstanding the historical claim of the Jewish people to the land, Palestine was an Arab country and that the Arabs within its boundaries needed to decide their fate without interference or direction from the Jewish population. But that rationale ignored the reality that Palestine's fate was never going to be determined by Zionism or Zionists, but by the so-called great powers of the world. The winding road followed by the great powers in reaching a proposed solution is discussed in the following chapter, and of course the whys and wherefores of how that proposed resolution to the conflict emerged are critical to the considerations that the reader can take into account in reaching a conclusion as to whether the creation of the State of Israel in 1948 was justifiable and just.

We know about the opposition of some portion of the Jewish community to the Zionist movement, but what about the sentiments of the non-Jewish world (aside from the Arabs)? The movement had been endorsed without reservation following its inception by many prominent non-Jewish men and women in the world. Non-Jews, when they spoke up on the subject of Zionism itself, generally commented that it represented a worthy ideal insofar as it marked the path to a promising future for those Jews seeking to make Palestine their home. But Zionism did not become a widespread topic in the non-Jewish world until roughly the start of World War I when non-Jews began to think through the situation of world Jewry in sociological terms rather than in the context of religion. This brings us back to the subject of the path pursued by the great powers to resolve Palestine's fate, to which we will turn later in these pages.

It is now time to examine the pertinent history of Zionism and the Palestine saga from 1920 through to 1948 when the modern State of Israel came into being. During the 1920's and into the 1930's, those Jews who arrived in Palestine found economic conditions offering the prospect of prosperity. Aside from occasional non-violent demonstrations by Palestinian Arabs, as well as periodic instances of violence instigated by the Palestinians, the Jewish immigrants continued to live in relative peace, if not perfect harmony, with Palestine's Arab inhabitants. The violence between Arabs and Jews during the decade of the 1920's was initially marked primarily by Arab terrorists' sporadic attacks at Jewish agricultural communities in the Galilee and several other locations during the first four months of 1920, resulting in a number of Jewish casualties. Riots erupted in Jerusalem in April 1920, with five Jews killed and scores injured. Then, in May 1921, Arab terrorists attacked Jews in Jaffa and murdered 27 Jews and injured well over 100. A new wave of Arab-instigated violence occurred in 1924, with scattered attacks targeting various Jewish communities killing 135 Jews and injuring more than 300. And then came four days of bloody riots and mob violence in Jerusalem, Hebron, and Safed in August 1929, all provoked by Arab clerics' and politicians' false allegations that Jews were plotting to take control of the Al-Aqsa Mosque on the Temple Mount in Jerusalem. The Arab violence began when Arab terrorists attacked Jews in Jerusalem, killing 47, and subsequently spread to other cities, including Hebron and then Safed. At least 65 Jews were slaughtered in Hebron, and 18 Jews were murdered in Safed. More than 100 Arabs were killed by the British during those four days of violence due to efforts by Great Britain to halt the massacre of Jews.

But there was another development in process that would have a consequential impact on the future relationship between the

Palestinians and Jews. Behind the scenes, there was an element of the Arab population that, commencing in the 1920's, had begun preparing for eventual armed struggle against the Jews in Palestine. This occurred on the basis that the Jewish immigrants were the enemy and that they were appropriating the land of Palestine to which the Arabs of Palestine were entitled (this charge is contradicted by the circumstance that the land acquired by the Jewish immigrants was always legally purchased). Instrumental in setting the tone and direction of Palestinian resistance to the Zionist presence was the Grand Mufti of Jerusalem, a rabid Jew-hater who emerged as a public figure in 1921 and dominated Palestinian politics for the next thirty years. With much evidence to support their viewpoint, there are those who posit that the Grand Mufti was the founding father of the rejectionist campaign against a Jewish presence in Palestine that continues to this day. Little was it perceived at the time that the Palestinian resistance forming in the 1920's, based on Islamic tenets and a growing antipathy toward Jewish immigrants, would presage the continuing Palestinian Arab opposition to the Jewish presence, and to the State of Israel that ensued. In response to violence instigated by the Arabs, the Jews were prompted in June 1920 to begin creating a self-defense organization that came to be known as the Haganah, that later evolved into the Israel Defense Forces, now commonly referred to as the IDF.

Commencing in the early 1930's, and throughout the first half of that decade, the Arab armed struggle against the Jews of Palestine was marked by the intermittent killing of Jewish farmers.

Notwithstanding those incidents, Jews continued to arrive in Palestine, and those who established their bona fides as residents were grateful for their mostly secure and flourishing surroundings. Simultaneously, elements of the Palestinian Arab community, aroused by the Arab press, encouraged the masses of Palestinians to engage in acts of incitement against the Jews by playing on the perceived injustice that the Zionists were causing the Palestinians to suffer. In April 1936, events took a dramatic turn as widespread violence against the Jews exploded across the landscape. Fires were set in fields. Orange groves were destroyed. Jews were slain by knives, stones, snipers' gunfire, and by pummeling carried out by Arab mobs. Jews were murdered in their beds at home, ambushed while traveling or while walking to or from work, and killed by bombs hurled onto trains and buses and streets filled with human activity. These acts of terror endured, whereas actions involving violence that had occurred in the 1920's were short-lived. It seemed to the Jews that the conflict was turning into an all-consuming confrontation. And of equal or greater concern, it was becoming clear to the Jews that they were now facing for the first time a sustained uprising being stirred up and supported by a nationalistic movement that was willing to be identified with the commission of ongoing terrorist acts. Many historians credit the Grand Mufti of Jerusalem with being the leader of the Palestinian national movement. He most certainly was instrumental in fomenting the violence against the Jews that commenced in 1936.

From April through July 1936, the Jews kept their response restrained. Only during August, after four months of devastating

Arab terror, did the Jews react by initiating acts of retaliation. Even after scores of Jews had been killed and wounded, the Jews were not thinking in terms of turning to military means to beat back the attacks. Nonetheless, the brutality of the events between April and July 1936 sent shock waves through the Jews in Palestine. The attacks clarified that the Jewish population could no longer ignore Arab nationalism, and that the nationalist movement was determined to halt the immigration of Jews to Palestine. The notion that the Palestinians were willing to live peacefully with the Zionists was dispelled. No longer would the Jews be deceived into believing that they could escape the vicious cycle of confrontations that was now in play. It was time for the Jews to assume the role of a combatant. Reality had set in.

The violence had quieted by the fall of 1936. It picked up again in October 1937, and now the Jews responded with violence of their own following each murderous act perpetrated by the Arabs. The number of Arab victims began to exceed the number of Jewish deaths. Jewish and Arab hostilities, marked by atrocities committed by both sides, continued through the latter months of 1938, the Jews finding particularly shocking an Arab massacre of Jews in Tiberias in October 1938 in which 21 Jews were killed, including ten children under the age of twelve. The number of deaths among Arabs continued to exceed Jewish fatalities in large part because many of the attacks upon Arabs were more deadly than those attributed to the Arabs. It is relevant to note that the attacks on the Jewish residents during the latter part of 1937 and during 1938 were supported by Arab leaders and the Palestinian masses. In contrast, the Zionist movement denounced the violence by Jews against Arabs (most of the Jewish terrorists belonged to marginal groups intent on attacking Arabs and who ignored or disrespected the official proclamations of the elected leadership of Palestine's Jews).

By early 1939, with World War II on the horizon and Britain anxious to curtail the Arab violence in Palestine, which was expressing itself against the British as well as the Jews, heavily reinforced British military forces had subdued the Arab fighters, ending at least for the time being the carnage committed against the Jews and casualties suffered by British troops. But the Jews remembered well the brutal conflict that ran from 1936 through 1939. The Zionists were resigned to the likelihood that a new round of attacks by the Arabs was on the horizon that would probably be no less brutal than those that had occurred during the prior four years, but no one could project a timeline. The question was not if the conflict would be renewed, but when. So in 1939, a general staff was assigned to the Haganah, which had been serving as a self-defense organization, and the process of building a Jewish army in the land of Palestine began in earnest. There could be little doubt that whenever the conflict over Palestine's fate started up again, the Jews would need to rely on armed strength to shield the Zionists from annihilation.

During the first half of the 1940's, the Zionist movement was primarily concerned with the possibility that British forces would leave Palestine, exposing the Jews to a Nazi-inspired revolt by the Palestinian Arabs, whose nationalistic fervor had now reached a new peak. This concern was an outgrowth of the fact that in November 1941, the Grand Mufti of Jerusalem (the same Grand Mufti who had been a leader of the Palestinian nationalistic movement cited earlier) met with Hitler in Germany. An official alliance was established between the Palestinian Arab movement, led by the Grand Mufti, and Nazi Germany. This threat of new turmoil receded in time. Still, at the conclusion of World War II, the Arab issue remained as the principal danger to the future of the Zionist project in Palestine. In early 1947 the British withdrew all their forces from Palestine because Britain was unwilling to continue subjecting its military to the persistent armed assaults by the Jews and Arabs. The United Nations was left to decide Palestine's fate. When the Palestinian Arabs rejected the proposed UN partition plan in November 1947, violence once again erupted throughout Palestine, marked by armed attacks on Jewish settlements, acts of sabotage, and ambushes of Jews traveling the territory's streets and roads. The savage war between the Jews and Palestinian Arabs, resulting in the death of close to 2,000 Jews, lasted from December 1947 until May 1948, when Britain relinquished its role as mandatory, and the State of Israel was proclaimed. And as the expression goes, the rest is history, a history which the Palestinians have always viewed with bitterness.

It is for you to determine whether the effect of the Zionist movement, as described above and notwithstanding Arab efforts over the years to whitewash the anti-Jewish violence that occurred in Palestine between 1920 and 1939, is an element of the complex whole that weighs in favor of or against the argument that the establishment of the State of Israel in the Middle East was justifiable and just. But I urge you not to rush to judgment one way or the other. A full array of further issues that need to be examined, both in the context of the Zionists' role and otherwise, is yet to be presented for consideration. Moving forward, try to keep in mind that the validity of Zionism was accepted and supported by international institutions that recognized the right of the Jews to national self-determination in Palestine based on historical ties to their homeland, and that those institutions, by so doing, confirmed international recognition of that right. Yes, Zionism can be a thorny subject for some people. Still, hopefully, you did not take the easy way out and gloss over the meaningful details set out above that apply to the story of the Zionist movement's role in the process leading to the creation of the State of Israel in May 1948. If you absorbed those details, perhaps you now grasp that Zionism was not and is not an evil or fiendish undertaking aimed at coercing the Palestinian Arabs into submission. Nothing about the Zionist movement or its project in Palestine should undermine the argumentation underlying the principle that Israel's establishment was justifiable and just.

CHAPTER 2:

The Revelant History - It Was What It Was

A short version of the history of the creation of the modern State of Israel would likely begin with reference to the issuance in 1917 by British Foreign Secretary Arthur Balfour of the Balfour Declaration, which declared, "His Majesty's government view with favour the establishment in Palestine of a national home for the Jewish people." That history would then move on to 1923, when the League of Nations adopted the identical concept and proclaimed its mandate for Palestine, to be administered by Great Britain. The League of Nations mandate was responsible for putting the words cited in the Balfour Declaration into effect. The history would then fast forward to 1947, when the United Nations voted in favor of partitioning Palestine into a Jewish state and an Arab state. The British mandate having ended, the Jews in Palestine accepted the partition plan and declared the creation of the independent State of Israel. The Palestinian Arabs rejected the plan and, in collaboration with the armies of five Arab countries, attacked Israel in what became known as Israel's War of Independence. Israel won that battle and survives today after prevailing in several subsequent wars with the Arabs.

If you were to rely on the adequacy of the above condensed history, you would be cheating yourself out of the opportunity to learn the full scope and critical details of the events leading to Israel's establishment. Not wanting you to suffer such a hurt, I will relate the complete story or at least the significant particulars of that history. Please be forewarned that if you read the following version of the history casually, i.e., without paying close attention to details I will describe, you will remain cheated. And more to the point, only if you care enough to weigh all the distinct features of the history in conjunction with your grasping the big picture, will you enable yourself to fairly judge the impact of the history on the issue of whether Israel's creation was just and justifiable.

Let's begin recounting the history with a discussion of the Balfour Declaration. This Declaration was a public statement issued by the British government during World War I announcing support for the establishment of a "national home for the Jewish people" in what was then a portion of the Ottoman Empire known as Palestine, which was then as now a nonexistent country. More precisely, the Balfour Declaration was a letter dated November 2, 1917, from British Foreign Secretary Arthur Balfour to Lord Walter Rothschild, a stalwart Zionist and a leader of Britain's Jewish community. It states that "His Majesty's government view with favour the establishment in

Palestine of a national home for the Jewish people." The full content of the letter is as follows:

Foreign Office, November 17th, 1917

Lord Rothschild,

I have much pleasure in conveying to you, on behalf of his Majesty's Government, the following declaration of sympathy with Jewish Zionist aspirations which has been submitted to, and approved by, the Cabinet: "His Majesty's Government view with favour the establishment in Palestine of a national home for the Jewish people, and will use their best endeavours to facilitate the achievement of this object, it being clearly understood that nothing shall be done which may prejudice the civil and religious rights of existing non-Jewish communities in Palestine, or the rights and political status enjoyed by Jews in any other country."

I should be grateful if you would bring this declaration to the knowledge of the Zionist Federation.

ARTHUR JAMES BALFOUR
Secretary of State for Foreign Affairs

Lord Rothschild, to whom the letter was addressed, described it as "the most important moment in Jewish history in the last 1,800 years." The Balfour Declaration marked the zenith in the first twenty years of the Zionist movement's life. The document was the most meaningful step ever undertaken up until that time in support of the idea of restoring Jewish self-determination (the right of a people to decide upon its political status or form of government without outside influence) in a land that the Jewish people deemed to be their historical national homeland. On December 7, 1917, only weeks after the issuance of the Balfour Declaration, British, Australian, and New Zealand forces drove from Palestine the Ottoman Empire, which had occupied the territory of Palestine for four centuries. Per the San Remo Resolution issued in 1920, and in accordance with the vote of the League of Nations in 1923, the Balfour Declaration was enshrined in international law, leading eventually to the passage of the 1947 UN partition plan and ultimately to the creation of the modern-day State of Israel on May 14, 1948.

It is key to recall that the path charted by the Zionists at the time of their movement's inception had not clarified how the existence of a Jewish homeland would be secured through international law or guarantees. But the Zionists always understood that the homeland's future in Palestine would need to be secured, and the Balfour Declaration opened the door to that outcome. Yes, the Belfour Declaration represented, in a broad sense, a meaningful diplomatic breakthrough for the Zionist movement. Still, in a narrower sense, it played no less critical a role insofar as it was to generate the much sought after legal cushion for the Zionist project.

Why did Great Britain issue the Balfour Declaration? Theories and suspicions abound. But the most likely reason that can be drawn from the literature bearing on the subject of the motives of the British government appears to be that Britain's war cabinet and Balfour himself (a staunch advocate for the Zionist movement) were searching for support for the Allied war effort, including from world Jewry. Additionally, Britain found the letter's words to be a meaningful way to give expression to the country's long-standing sympathy for the Zionist undertaking to establish a homeland in Palestine. But as far as I am concerned, the motive or motives behind the issuance of the Balfour Declaration, whatever they may have been, are not germane to the issue of whether the creation of Israel was justifiable and just. One can argue until blue in the face that the thinking behind the Declaration was prompted by ill will towards the Palestinian Arabs. This certainly does not appear to have been a consideration in Britain's thinking. But what does the motive(s) matter one way or another in the context of this book's theme? What needs to be considered is whether the objective of the document was to achieve a constructive or positive result in light of all the surrounding circumstances. If that is the conclusion drawn, then that would very well lend considerable support to the proposition that the Balfour Declaration was part of a history that depicts Israel's establishment as justifiable and just.

But before moving along to a discussion of the San Remo Resolution and subsequent relevant historical events, it is necessary to cover two other issues related to the Balfour Declaration. The first is that of the Palestinian Arabs' reaction, or at least of their political leaders and spokespersons, to the Declaration.

They were not impressed by the fact that Great Britain, the greatest world power of the time, had recognized the right of the Jewish people to a homeland in Palestine. Ever since the issuance of the Balfour Declaration, and right up until today, the leaders of the Palestinian Arabs have lambasted the document as illegitimate, invalid, an historic mistake, a disgrace, a disaster, a catastrophe, a betrayal, a crime against humanity, a crime against the Palestinian people, a despicable plot, etc. (the list of mean-spirited references and slurs could extend for pages). In an address to the United Nations General Assembly on September 22, 2016, Mahmoud Abbas, President of the Palestinian Authority, asserted, "One hundred years have passed since the notorious Balfour Declaration, by which Britain gave, without any right, authority or consent from anyone, the land of Palestine to another people." Of course, Abbas distorted the meaning and intent of the Balfour Declaration. It gave nothing to anyone. It simply recognized the right of the Jews to seek a homeland in Palestine. In that same speech at the UN, Abbas attempted to exact an apology from the British, a demand that was categorically rejected.

The Palestinians, in short, have never been able or willing to accept the Balfour Declaration as an attempt to bestow national self-determination on a people who had what they (the Jews) and others (certainly including the British) considered to be an intimate 3,000 year or so connection with the land of Palestine. Instead, the ongoing Palestinian campaign against the Declaration is founded on the argument that it gave birth to the conflict that persists to this day. That campaign has become part of the effort to delegitimize Israel's existence and has helped thwart attempts to resolve the Israel-Palestinian conflict. The Balfour Declaration continues to be mourned by the Palestinians, and much of the Arab world, as the initial step leading to what they view as the calamitous creation of the State of Israel.

The second issue that requires consideration is whether the Balfour Declaration rose to the level of a legally binding declaration since it was not an agreement between two nations, but instead was in the form of a letter in which the British government unilaterally acknowledged the right of the Jewish people to a national homeland in Palestine. It is a common understanding among nations, and an accepted principle of international law, that a unilateral declaration that is officially issued by a government that intends it to be binding creates a legal obligation on the part of the issuing government that must be honored by that country and that must be respected by the international community. The Balfour Declaration was officially backed by Britain's war cabinet and was issued by the British Foreign Secretary (who clearly was authorized to bind Britain in such matters). Nothing contained in the document indicated or suggested that the British government was not intending to be bound by the letter's seemingly unambiguous language. Accordingly, the Balfour Declaration was generally viewed as a legally binding pronouncement. And the judgment that the Balfour Declaration deserved legally binding status was reinforced several years later when it was incorporated into documents that were binding under the tenets of international law.

Following the defeat of the Ottoman Empire in World War I, the Allies — the four principal allied powers involved in the war, Great Britain, France, Italy, and Japan — convened in San Remo, Italy in April 1920 to give structure to the Middle Eastern territories that had been part of that former empire for the prior 400 years. The practice of slicing up conquered land was one in which governments had commonly engaged throughout world history. In formulating the process leading to what was to become the map of the modern Middle East, the ultimate goal of the Allies was to establish a group of Arab nations, which had never before existed, and a national home for the Jewish people. The process, designed to adhere to the principle of self-determination, which meant those newly-independent populations would be self-governing, involved a mentoring program referred to as mandates. Mandates were established for three former Ottoman territories. It was decided that the portion of the former Ottoman Empire that was to form the mandate for Palestine's territory should be held in trust by Great Britain (as a country assigned to administer a mandate, Britain was referred to as a mandatory). That mandate included an area east of the Jordan River (what is today Jordan) as well as all the land west of the Jordan River between the Jordan and the Mediterranean Sea (what is today the State of Israel plus the area presently referred to by some as the West Bank and by others as Judea and Samaria), and the Gaza Strip. This was the landmass in the Middle East where a national home for the Jewish people was to be created, it being commonly understood, then as now, that the term "national home" referred to the concept of a nation.

The mandates were to be carried out until a particular territory was able to self-rule as a state, at which juncture that mandate would end. Britain's role as mandatory included, among other administrative responsibilities, processing Jewish immigration into Palestine. Interestingly, and of pivotal impact, the Palestine mandate did not recite a protocol for establishing a national home for the Jewish people in Palestine. Rather, it was determined at San Remo that it would be left to the Jews to facilitate the actual implementation of the Balfour Declaration's promise to support the establishment of a Jewish homeland in Palestine. As history has recorded, that implementation occurred on May 14, 1948, the day on which Prime Minister David Ben-Gurion proclaimed the birth of the modern State of Israel. But I am getting ahead of myself.

On April 26, 1920, the four Allied powers signed the San Remo Resolution. This document had the effect of converting the Balfour Declaration into a binding international understanding bearing upon the establishment of a Jewish national home in the territory where Britain had been assigned as the mandatory. As mandatory for Palestine, Britain was tasked with effectuating "…the declaration initially made on November 2, 1917, by the British Government, and adopted by the Other Allied Powers…." The complete wording of the San Remo Resolution read, in pertinent part, as follows:

> The Mandatory will be responsible for putting into effect the declaration originally made on November 2, 1917, by the British Government, and adopted by the

Other Allied Powers, in favour of the establishment in Palestine of a national home for the Jewish people, it being clearly understood that nothing shall be done which may prejudice the civil and religious rights of existing non-Jewish communities in Palestine, or the rights and political status enjoyed by Jews in any other country.

The mandate for Palestine formulated at San Remo, which straightforwardly relied on the Balfour Declaration as its foundation, was ratified by the Council of the League of Nations, the predecessor to the United Nations, on July 24, 1922. The League of Nations mandate for Palestine reiterated that Great Britain was assigned the powers of mandatory over Palestine's territory. The League of Nations Council, composed of permanent members Great Britain, France, Italy, and Japan and non-permanent members Belgium, Brazil, Greece, and Spain, incorporated the following clauses in the preamble to the League of Nations mandate:

Whereas the Principal Allied Powers have also agreed that the Mandatory should be responsible for putting into effect the declaration originally made on November 2nd, 1917, by the government of his Britannic Majesty and adopted by the said Powers, in favor of the establishment in Palestine of a national home for the Jewish people, it being clearly understood that nothing should be done which might prejudice the civil and religious rights of existing non-Jewish communities in Palestine, or the rights and political status enjoyed by Jews in any other country; and

Whereas recognition has thereby been given to the historical connection of the Jewish people with Palestine and to the grounds for reconstituting their national home in that country.

The League of Nations mandate was unanimously ratified in 1923 by the 56 member nations of the League of Nations. It put the resolution adopted at San Remo into practice. Moreover, it was a formal declaration to the world that the creation of a Jewish homeland in Palestine was in the offing. I need to emphasize that what transpired at San Remo in 1920 and subsequently at the League of Nations in 1922-23, all as described above, involved the recognition and then ratification by the international community of the Jewish people's right to a homeland in Palestine. Those events established the legal foundation for the creation of the State of Israel. They ordained the borders of that nation-to-be. And together, they were incorporated into instruments of international law. There can be no denying that what was crafted at San Remo and approved by the League of Nations emerged as international law under any definition of that term. Of no less significance, the law that evolved acknowledged the Jewish people's historical connection with Palestine as the grounds for reconstituting a national home for the Jews in that land. It was that historical connection that had been at the heart of the Balfour Declaration and been recognized in the resolution issued at San Remo. The legal right assigned to the Jews at San Remo to restore a Jewish homeland in Palestine, and which was ratified by the League of Nations, has never been cancelled, repealed, or annulled by any authority or entity. It is not a settled matter that international law would permit such a reversal even if it had ever been sought.

Although it appeared that the intention at San Remo was to include all of Palestine in the mandate for that territory, Great Britain, before the unanimous ratification of the mandate for Palestine by the members of the League of Nations in 1923, took advantage of a legal loophole and severed the entire area east of the Jordan River, giving it to the Hashemite clan of Arabs in gratitude for the support offered to the Allied war effort. The Hashemites proceeded to create the kingdom of Transjordan (subsequently renamed Jordan). The separated area, the majority of whose residents were Arabs who had roots in Palestine, represented roughly 78 percent of the territory contemplated by the League of Nations to compose its mandate for Palestine. Notwithstanding that many objective people have made the argument over the years that what is today Jordan should be considered the home of the Palestinian Arabs (and that therefore a two-state solution to the conflict has already been effectuated, the Arab state being Jordan and the Jewish state being Israel), I have chosen for two reasons not to adopt or pursue that line of thinking. First, there is some difference of opinion, among those who have examined the issue, as to whether the commitment expressed in the Balfour Declaration in support of a Jewish homeland in Palestine was intended to include as part of that homeland the portion of Palestine east of the Jordan River. Second, is the conclusion I reached that it does not serve any valid purpose to press the position that Jordan is the home of the Palestinian Arabs given that I do not see what bearing the formation of the country that is today Jordan had or has on the specific question of whether the establishment of the State of Israel was justifiable and just.

The next link in the chain of historical events occurred in 1937 when Lord Earl Peel traveled to the Middle East at the request of Britain's Parliament. Parliament had appointed a royal commission of inquiry, headed by Lord Peel, to attempt to identify how to satisfy Arab complaints and demands surrounding Jewish immigration to Palestine. The Peel Commission Report concluded that the only solution to resolving the conflicting claims of the Jews and Arabs to the land of Palestine was to partition Palestine into separate Jewish and Arab states. The Peel partition plan proposed that the Arabs living in the area west of the Jordan River would receive approximately 85 percent of that territory. The Jews would obtain the remaining 15 percent. The land would be divided based on the number of Jews and Arabs living in particular locations. In other words, the Jews were being offered 15 percent of the mandate for Palestine that was still in place after Britain gave the land east of the Jordan River to the Arabs. The Zionists were disheartened that the plan recommended that they come into possession of only 15 percent of the slightly more than 10,000 square miles of what remained of the Palestine mandate. Still, they agreed to further negotiations with the British. The Arabs rejected the plan on the basis that the offer of land to them was inadequate, and refused to discuss any possible compromises. Had the Palestinians accepted the Peel Commission plan, the Palestinian Arabs would have obtained a state in 1937 that would have included somewhere in the vicinity of 85 (eighty-five) percent of mandatory Palestine. Perhaps the Palestinians' refusal to accept the Peel partition plan was the basis for the origination of the oft-heard remark, immortalized by former Israel Foreign Minister and Ambassador to the UN Abba Eban, that the Palestinians never miss an opportunity to miss an opportunity.

Now we move to the historical role played by the United Nations, which succeeded the League of Nations in 1945. Like the League of Nations, the UN was an international organization of nations pledged to promote world peace and security and maintain treaty obligations and the observance of international law. Formed under a permanent charter ratified by 50 countries, the UN recognized its responsibility to perpetuate existing rights of countries as established in previously enacted international agreements. To that end, Article 80 of the UN Charter stated:

> . . . nothing in this Chapter shall be construed in or of itself to alter in any manner the rights whatsoever of any states or any peoples or the terms of existing international instruments to which members of the United Nations may respectively be parties.

The impact of Article 80 was to reaffirm the legally binding nature of the Balfour Declaration, and to ensure the rights of the Jewish people that had been expressed in the San Remo

Resolution and then confirmed by the international community as a result of the unanimous ratification by the League of Nations in 1923 of its mandate for Palestine.

Following the end of World War II, the British attempted to work out an understanding between the Jews and Palestinian Arabs, but concluded that the challenge was insurmountable due to the unwillingness of the Arabs to accept the presence of a Jewish state in their midst and of the Jews to agree to any arrangement that did not result in the creation of a Jewish state. So Britain dropped the matter into the lap of the UN in February 1947. The UN wasted no time setting up a Special Commission on Palestine that was assigned the daunting task of finding a way to resolve the impasse. Delegates from eleven nations (Australia, Canada, Czechoslovakia, Guatemala, India, Iran, the Netherlands, Peru, Sweden, Uruguay, and Yugoslavia) were dispatched to the Middle East to investigate possible solutions. All eleven delegates concluded that the conflicting territorial claims of the Jews and Arabs were irreconcilable. The delegates of seven nations (Canada, Czechoslovakia, Guatemala, the Netherlands, Peru, Sweden, and Uruguay) recommended the establishment of two separate states, one Arab and one Jewish, with Jerusalem to be an international city administered by the UN. Delegates from three nations (India, Iran, and Yugoslavia) urged the formation of a unitary state consisting of Arab and Jewish provinces, and Australia abstained.

Palestine's Jews were displeased about the amount of territory offered to them by the Special Commission, and the recommendation that Jerusalem, with its large Jewish population, not be part of the Jewish nation. But they were willing to accept the proposal. The Arabs, on the other hand, rejected the Special Commission's plan. An ad hoc committee of the UN General Assembly was then called upon to consider the matter further. That committee rejected the Arab demand for a unitary Arab state and agreed that the Special Commission's majority recommendation that two separate states be created represented the fairest solution. On November 29, 1947, the UN General Assembly, by a vote of 33 for, 13 against, and ten abstentions, adopted the partition plan proposed by the Special Commission's majority. Among the countries voting in favor of partition were France, the USSR, and the United States. Among the 13 countries voting against the partition plan were Afghanistan, Egypt, Iran, Iraq, Lebanon, Pakistan, Saudi Arabia, Syria, Turkey, and Yemen (no surprises there!). Great Britain and China were among the ten countries that abstained. There have been those who have sliced and diced the UN vote to belittle the outcome, but obviously, a clear majority of the then UN member countries supported the partition plan. Unfortunately, a huge problem still remained after the UN General Assembly approved the partition plan, that being the absence of a protocol for implementing the plan as a solution to the conflict in the face of Arab opposition to any Jewish self-determination, even in an area of Palestine where Jews were a majority.

The UN partition plan was based solely on population distribution. No consideration whatsoever was given to matters of security. The Jewish state was to be approximately 5,500 square miles, with the Arab state to be approximately 4,500 square miles. Roughly 60 percent of what was to become the Jewish state was the Negev desert, believed at the time to be uninhabitable and unsuitable for any agriculture. According to official UN estimates, the Jewish state's population was to be 538,000 Jews and 397,000 Arabs, and the Arab state was to be populated by 804,000 Arabs and 10,000 Jews. The proposal that Jerusalem be internationalized meant that the 100,000 or so Jews in Jerusalem would not be included as part of the Jewish state. In essence, the UN plan was intended to divide the territory of Palestine as it existed in 1947 in order to grant to the Jewish majority, in the area allocated to the Jewish state, the right of self-determination, and to do likewise for the Arab majority in the area allocated to an Arab state.

The UN resolution recommending the partition plan was advisory rather than mandatory since it was passed by the UN General Assembly, not by the UN Security Council. The Palestinians were quick to reject the UN partition plan, thus again turning their backs on an offer of a state and the opportunity to self-govern. Violence erupted throughout Palestine following the Palestinians' rejection of the partition plan, and ultimately the birth of the State of Israel was proclaimed on May 14, 1948, in the area assigned to the Jews by the UN plan. Israel's War of Independence then began when the armies of five Arab countries invaded the new State of Israel virtually immediately (within hours) upon it becoming a state. The ensuing war ended in February 1949 with a cease-fire. Inasmuch as no Arab state was willing to recognize the Jewish state or sign a peace agreement, the cease-fire agreement provided that the cease-fire lines simply represented the opposing forces' positions at the time hostilities ceased but were not to be construed as territorial borders. This suited the Arabs perfectly because borders suggest a land's permanence whereas cease-fire lines do not, and the Arabs envisioned that the war to destroy Israel would resume at some point. As we all know, the Palestinians have never accepted Israel's presence where it now stands on the world map, which is to say that the Palestinians have never agreed to any national borders for Israel. By the way, Israel was admitted to membership in the UN in 1949 as its fifty-ninth member.

What does the above history say about whether Israel was justifiably and justly created? I believe that the history I have set out proves the justifiability and justness of Israel's establishment. That history points to the inescapable conclusion that at the heart of the ultimate achievement of the Zionist movement were (a) the historical connection of the Jewish people to Palestine, and (b) the confirmation of the legal right of the Jewish people to a homeland in Palestine as reinforced in instruments of international law. What more supportive evidence could one want to prove the justifiability and justness of Israel's creation? Starting with the Balfour Declaration, and then taking into account the San Remo Resolution, the League of Nations mandate for Palestine, Article 80 of the UN Charter, and the vote of the UN General Assembly favoring partition, Israel's creation was based on a strong foundation. It was entirely legitimate, certainly no less so than the creation of most other countries. The strong foundation to which I have just referred reflects the international community's reaffirmation of the historic connection of the Jewish people to the area that is now Israel, and the conferring of that area to the Jewish people as the site of its future state. That strong foundation also reflects as much legal weight, as represented by instruments of international law, as does the right to exist of most other nations. And we have yet to consider, but will do so in due course, the details explaining how Israel's foundation is reinforced by the historical link of the Jewish people with the land of Palestine and how archeological findings prove that connection. That connection is, of course, the same one that convinced the international community, as represented by the League of Nations and then the United Nations, to support a Jewish state in Palestine.

Not only is it my view that the creation of Israel was based on as strong a foundation as was the founding of most other countries, but there is one particular aspect of the history that deserves special mention as the wrap-up to this chapter, and that relates to the relatively peaceful progression of the Zionist enterprise. It is beyond question that most nations have been born due to conquest, or at the least been subjected to episodes of violence and bloodshed during the course of their birth process. As anyone even remotely familiar with world history is aware, the Middle East has been subject to invasion and conquest from all directions forever. The land that is today Israel has not escaped that pattern of turmoil. And not surprisingly, the Palestinian Arabs, in an effort to parlay the just described violence angle to their advantage, have lamented for many decades that the Zionists forced hundreds of thousands of Palestinians from their homes in the land of Palestine in 1948 in the months before and during Israel's War of Independence, an allegation that is offered as an explanation for why the Palestinians continue to reject Israel's legitimacy and right to exist as a sovereign nation (the charge that the Jews engaged in purposeful behavior that produced the flood of Palestinian refugees in 1948, causing them to be unfairly dispossessed of their homes, will be closely examined and refuted in an upcoming chapter).

However, if you carefully consider the history I have set forth, you will hopefully agree that in relative terms, the Zionist project progressed peacefully. It was not a hostile invasion by Jews into the land of Palestine. True, the history described was marked by instances of violence, and one period (1936-39) of prolonged violent conflict. Still, one needs to carefully examine who initiated or provoked the violence. Please consider that the Zionists were engaged in reclaiming the land, not in conquering it. The reclaimed land had been legally purchased on the open market, not stolen by violent means. The Jews who immigrated to Palestine were not invaders, but people returning to their ancestral homeland. They had no military capability to speak of until after it came time to fight their War of Independence in 1948, a battle precipitated by the unprovoked invasion of the newly-formed State of Israel by the armies of five Arab countries who were seeking Israel's annihilation. Overall history reflects a non-violent approach by the Zionists towards the Palestinian Arabs except when provoked to retaliate for Arab violence against the Jews, all of which lends support to the determination that Israel was created with justification and justly. The Zionists built their country not through violence aimed at the Arabs, but based on their ancient connection to Palestine.

CHAPTER 3:

What Does Size Have to Do With It?

I recognize that the question I raise in this book, namely whether the establishment of the State of Israel in 1948 was justifiable and just, needs to be resolved primarily based on fact-driven evidence. Feelings and emotions should not enter into the picture to any significant extent. But just as it is necessary when viewing historical events to go beyond the mere facts and reflect upon the meaning of those facts in a way that gives the history a human side, so too is it essential to go beyond the facts to evaluate the equities and fairness of any possible outcome before drawing a final conclusion. With that premise in mind, I want to comment upon a purely geographical feature of Israel — the country's size.

Israel is a small country, being roughly the size of the state of New Jersey. Israel is five percent of the size of the state of California. It is some 290 miles in length and about 85 miles across at its widest point. It is nine miles wide (no, that is not a misprint) at its narrowest point, and is only 40 miles wide where the Jordan River flows closest to the Mediterranean Sea.

The country of Israel is but a speck on the world map, consisting of about 0.2 percent of the amount of land possessed by the Arab world. It represents approximately one percent of the area that was allotted to establish Arab countries on territory that had been occupied by the Ottoman Empire. Inasmuch as there are presently 22 Arab states, all blessed with sovereignty, where is the equity, where is the fairness, in not accepting the presence of one small Jewish state in the Jewish people's ancestral homeland? When looked at from the perspective of Israel's size, how can one take the position that Israel's creation was not justifiable and just? Enough said!

CHAPTER 4:

An Arab Majority in Palestine - Did That Matter?

World leaders who were spearheading or otherwise actively supporting efforts to provide for the Jewish people's self-determination in their ancestral homeland knew full well that the land of Palestine did not at that juncture in history contain a majority Jewish population. For that reason, among others, the Palestinian Arabs were urging that the only logical outcome to the conflict was the establishment of a unitary Arab state. However, the decision to support the creation of a national home for the Jewish people in Palestine was prompted not by a consideration of demographics, but by recognition of the Jews' historical ties to the land of Palestine.

Keep in mind that the series of declarations, resolutions, and treaties issued from 1917 through 1923 reiterated the historical link of the Jews with Palestine as the basis for backing the creation of a Jewish homeland in Palestine. These same world leaders who were "pushing" for a Jewish state must have also understood that the claim of the Zionists to self-determination was as compelling as that of the Arab people, who had lived stateless for 400 years under the yoke of the Ottoman Empire. They pushed even though the Arabs had outnumbered the Jews in Palestine as a whole going back to the time of the Arab conquest in the 7th century. When the UN partition plan finally evolved in 1947, approximately 1.2 million Arabs resided in Palestine versus roughly 600,000 Jews.

But, and this is a very big "but," the Jews were a clear majority in 1947 in the area offered to the Jews by the UN plan. There were 538,000 Jews versus 397,000 Arabs within the frontiers of the proposed new state, and the Jewish population of Jerusalem exceeded the number of Arab residents of that city. Also, let's not lose sight of the fact that the Arab population of Palestine grew enormously beginning in the 1920's. This happened once Arabs residing in various parts of what had been the Ottoman Empire began migrating to Palestine, drawn by the growing prosperity of the territory resulting from the Zionist project.

On the other hand, the Jews never had a fair shot at becoming the majority population in Palestine as a whole due to the restrictive policies imposed by the British mandatory on Jewish immigration commencing in 1939. As a result of those policies, Arabs from anywhere and everywhere were welcome to migrate to Palestine from the year 1939 onward. But Jews were stymied from doing the same. Who is to say that if the Jews and Arabs had been afforded an equal opportunity to come to Palestine from 1939 to 1947, that the Jews would not have outnumbered the Arabs in Palestine by 1947?

Again, it needs to be emphasized that the partition plan approved by the UN in November 1947 was not grounded on population considerations. It was founded upon the international consensus that the Jews were deserving of a homeland in the land of Palestine due to the historical ties of the Jewish people to that land. But is there anyone who really believes that the Palestinians would have compromised with the Jews over the seemingly irreconcilable territorial claims of the two sides even if the Jews had outnumbered the Arabs in 1947 in all of Palestine? Please do not spend any time trying to assess whether the Palestinians would have relented in 1947 in their objection to a homeland being created for the Jews in Palestine, even if the Jews had been the majority in all of Palestine. To do so would serve no meaningful purpose. I say that because the fact that the Jews did not outnumber the Arabs in the whole of Palestine in 1947 is a "red herring" diverting attention from the overriding consideration, which is that the Jews were a clear majority in the area offered to them by the UN partition plan, which area became the State of Israel on May 14, 1948. And that Jewish majority was not established by removing or resettling Arabs. So whatever was the proportion of Arabs to Jews in all of Palestine is not a factor that should militate against the argument that Israel's establishment was justifiable and just.

CHAPTER 5:

Was the Creation of Israel Driven by the Holocaust?

Palestinians often reject the creation of Israel on the basis, among other grounds, that the country came into existence because of the Holocaust, the insinuation being that Israel came into being as compensation to the Jews for their suffering during the Holocaust, or that guilt on the part of nations that stood by while the Holocaust occurred was what motivated support for Israel's birth, or that the European powers created Israel in order to soothe their collective consciences due to the Holocaust having been perpetrated "right under their noses." Of course, if you paid close attention to the earlier description of historical events leading up to Israel's creation in 1948, and hopefully even if you did not absorb all of the details of that history, you would know that Israel's birth had nothing to do with the Holocaust. Rather, it had everything to do with (a) the achievements of the Zionist movement, which formally initiated the Zionist project in 1897, (b) the international recognition of the 3,000 year link of the Jewish people to the land of Palestine, in connection with which the momentum started building with the issuance of the Balfour Declaration in 1917, and (c) the acknowledgment by the world community of the legal right of the Jews to a homeland in Palestine, as expressed in 1920 in the San Remo Resolution and then confirmed by the unanimous vote of the League of Nations in 1923 establishing the mandate for Palestine. All of these historical circumstances occurred years before Hitler ascended to power in Germany.

To portray Israel's birth as being a result of the Holocaust, the origins of which did not begin to take shape until the 1930's, is to deny the role of the Zionists, to refuse to recognize the historical ties between the Jewish people and the land of Palestine, and to ignore the international treaties that established the legal right of world Jewry to a homeland in Palestine. It is, of course, true that when World War II ended and the scope and magnitude of the Holocaust became more evident, the goal of locating a sanctuary for Holocaust survivors was accelerated. This was no doubt accounting for a hastening of diplomatic moves leading to the 1947 UN partition plan. But that is not to concede that Israel exists in any measure because of the Holocaust. What is the justification for the Holocaust being asserted by the Palestinians as a reason to attack Israel's legitimacy or existence? There is none. It would appear that any such allegation represents yet another failed attempt to rationalize the rejection of the country's legitimacy and very existence, and certainly does not seem to undercut the argument that Israel's establishment was both justifiable and just.

CHAPTER 6:

Is Israel an Apartheid State?

What about the Palestinian Arabs' claims that the rejection of Israel's legitimacy and existence is well-founded because the country is an apartheid state and was born through the exercise of brutal ethnic cleansing? The ethnic cleansing charge grows from the creation of the mass of Palestinian refugees who fled their homes in 1948, both before and during Israel's War of Independence. The subject of the Palestinian refugees will be covered in detail in an upcoming chapter, so I will not address the accusation of ethnic cleansing for the time being.

As for the claim that Israel is an apartheid state, let's consider the elements of an apartheid state. In apartheid South Africa, blacks were not allowed to vote, enter white neighborhoods or municipal parks, mix with whites on beaches, or receive medical treatment at hospitals serving whites. They were forced to live in impoverished autonomous homelands called "Bantustans." They could not marry whites, attend white schools, use the same public restrooms as whites, or sit with whites on public transport. None of these restrictions apply to Arab citizens of Israel. Apartheid is marked by systemic racism and the absolute denial of fundamental human rights that evolve from apartheid legislation of the sort that South Africa enacted in abundance. Israel has never adopted any such laws or decrees.

And unlike blacks who lived in apartheid South Africa, Israeli Arabs serve in Israel's parliament, the Knesset. There are Arab judges, including those who have served on Israel's Supreme Court. Many Arabs live in the same communities as Jews in Israel. Roughly 20 percent of the students at Israel's universities are Arabs, and tenured Arab professors teach at those universities. Arab doctors and nurses compose about 20 percent of the medical staff at Israeli hospitals. Arabs serve with distinction in law enforcement and the Israel military, including in positions of command. And Arabs serve in Israel's diplomatic corps.

To charge Israel with being an apartheid state is akin to asserting that the moon is made out of cheese. It is a charge that is beyond inaccurate. It is nonsense. It can have only one purpose — to demonize Israel's very existence. A South African black, who had lived under apartheid in his homeland, noted during a visit to Israel that the only sign of South African style apartheid he found in the Jewish state was the impediment faced by Jews wishing to pray at the Temple Mount.

Israel's political leaders did not, in 1948 or subsequent to then, ever promote any system of discrimination against non-Jews. On the contrary, since its founding in 1948, Israel has grappled with how best to ensure that its Arab minority is afforded all of the legal and democratic rights available to its Jewish citizens. All citizens of Israel, totalling 9.3 million as of the end of 2020, of whom approximately 74% are Jewish, 21% are Arab, and 5% are non-Arab Christians or people of other religions, are treated as full-fledged citizens entitled to the complete range of civil and political rights available to the Jewish population. Those rights include voting in free elections, freedom of assembly, freedom of religion, freedom of speech, freedom of the press, and the right to an education equal to that received by Jews. Israeli democracy has its flaws and imperfections, but it is a democracy that is devoid of an apartheid state's characteristics. And no one should be fooled by the well-known reality that for those Palestinians who did not flee from their homes in the months before or during Israel's War of Independence, integration into Israeli society has been marked by blemishes and shortcomings. Israeli Arabs are the beneficiaries of educational and economic opportunities, to say nothing of basic freedoms, about which those living in Arab countries can only dream. Just try and tell an Arab citizen of Israel that they may lose their citizenship in Israel. You will surely be met by consternation, if not outright opposition to any such possibility.

Is there discrimination in Israel? Yes, sadly, there is. Some Israeli Jews discriminate against Arabs, just as some Israeli Jews discriminate against other Israeli Jews. Neither Israel nor its citizens are perfect. But name a country in this world where discrimination does not exist at all.

Of course, Arabs who live in the West Bank are often not treated as equals of the Jews who live there. However, the West Bank is an occupied territory (some prefer to call it a disputed territory) that potentially presents grave security risks to Israel (think Gaza!). I would like to suggest that any second-class treatment accorded to Arabs in the West Bank would vanish in not too many heartbeats were the Palestinians to acknowledge the legitimacy and existence of the State of Israel and that a negotiated peace with Israel is the logical course to pursue.

Let me conclude this chapter with a quote from Palestine Authority leader Mahmoud Abbas, who stated in 2013 concerning any future founding of a Palestinian state, "In a final resolution, we would not see the presence of a single Israeli – civilian or soldier, on our lands." If anything smacks of apartheid, it is that 2013 remark by Abbas. But I do not want to get sidetracked on the matter of tendencies of Palestinian Arabs to promote and engage in apartheid practices. The charge that Israel is an apartheid state falls within the category of bogus accusations that attempt to justify the rejection by the Palestinians of Israel's legitimacy and existence. It does nothing to detract from the argument that Israel's establishment was justifiable and just.

CHAPTER 7:

Is Israel a Racist Nation?

Is Israel a racist nation whose presence in the Middle East as the home of the Jewish people is deserving of rejection by the Palestinians? For starters, close to two million Arabs live in Israel, and for the most part, they peacefully coexist with Israel's Jewish citizens. Arabs normally interact with Jews daily. They are not confined to living in designated Arab areas. They are free to move into Jewish neighborhoods, where many Israeli Arabs have lived and presently live.

Also, one needs to keep in mind that more than half of the Jews who live in Israel are refugees or descendants of refugees from the Middle East and Northern Africa. These refugees arrived from nations such as Syria, Libya, Morocco, Tunisia, Egypt, Yemen, Algeria, and Iraq following the birth of Israel in May 1948. It is also the case that at about the time the initial wave of European Jewish refugees was immigrating to Palestine in the 1880's and 1890's, many Jewish refugees from Arab/Muslim countries were also beginning to arrive in Palestine to escape persecution. Those immigrants to Israel and their descendants were and are mostly people of color, not white Europeans. It can be accurately stated that Israel has a non-white majority.

Also, beginning during the 1980's, Israel has assisted more than 120,000 Ethiopians, all people of color, to start new lives in Israel. The total number of people of Ethiopian descent living today in Israel is close to 150,000. The first group of Ethiopian immigrants was composed of Ethiopian Jews known as Beta Israel. The second group of Ethiopian immigrants has been part of the Falash Mura community, whose members claim to be descendants of Jews who converted to Christianity generations ago under duress but now wish to return to Judaism. In the summer of 2020 there were approximately 8,000 Falash Mura still in Ethiopia anticipating their future immigration to Israel.

As discussed in the previous chapter dealing with apartheid, anyone who is present at any Israeli hospital will witness Arab and Jewish doctors and nurses treating both Arab and Jewish patients. A racist society would not tolerate a health system that treats everyone, both staff and patients, equally.

It is fair to say that Israelis are not indifferent to racism. Most recognize that racism stains a country's image. Nonetheless, there are Israeli Jews, as there are people in all countries, who are guilty of discriminatory behavior against others based on race. But the fact is that the majority of Israel's Jewish inhabitants are people of color who, together with Jews from Western and Eastern Europe, Arab Muslims, Arab and non-Arab

Christians, Druze, Bedouins, and others, compose one of the most diverse populations of any country on earth. So to brand the State of Israel as racist is to assert a falsehood of the most malicious sort. It is just another in the long list of unfounded rationalizations offered by the Palestinians for rejecting the legitimacy and existence of Israel. And it certainly does not lessen the validity of the argument that Israel's establishment was justifiable and just.

One final note is in order. Accusations of racial discrimination coming from Israel's Ethiopian community have brought the issue of anti-Ethiopian discrimination in Israel into the public eye in recent years. Israel is also confronted by recurring charges from Israeli Arabs that systemic racism exists in the country, particularly with respect to employment opportunities and the allocation of taxpayer dollars for educational needs and infrastructure improvements. There can be no doubt that such instances of racism do occur, notwithstanding that Israel's government attempts in good faith to effectively enforce Israeli laws that prohibit discrimination based on race and incitement to racism. The struggle to eliminate racial discrimination in Israel is ongoing — more and more Israelis are becoming aware that the problem is a plague upon every society, including their own.

CHAPTER 8:

Is Either Zionism or Israel a Creature of Colonialism?

Depending on who is charging that the Zionists were colonialists, or that Israel was created by a colonial power, the accusation is likely to proceed along one or more of the following lines in the effort to justify the rejection by the Palestinians of Israel's legitimacy and right to exist:

a) the Zionists were acting on behalf of colonialism and a colonial power(s);

b) Jews came to Palestine as European colonialists;

c) the idealistic socialism of the majority of the Jews who emigrated to Palestine was a cover intended to divert attention from the colonialist nature of the Zionist movement;

d) Israel represents the essence of European colonialism in the Middle East;

e) Israel has colonialist roots as a result of its nexus to the British mandate;

f) Israel is a colonial power;

g) Israel is a European colony backed by a foreign power(s) against the will of those populating the Middle East;

h) Israel is a colonial state guilty of imposing European values upon the Palestinian Arabs;

i) a colonial power(s) implanted Israel in the heart of the Muslim world;

j) a colonial power(s) was the principal force behind Israel's creation; and/or

k) colonial powers (Great Britain and the United States in particular) used the Jewish people as a tool to gain control in the Middle East to steal the natural resources of the Arab countries.

However, the facts of the matter, which militate against the accuracy of the arguments set out above to the effect that Zionism and Israel are colonialist creations, are numerous and resonate with the force of reason. In no particular order, the arguments supporting the conclusion that colonialism was not a factor in the Zionist movement or the establishment of Israel include the following:

a) there is no record or evidence that the Zionist movement ever sought aid (other than verbal support for the principle of a Jewish homeland in Palestine) from any colonial power, or from the government of any other country for that matter;

b) the Zionists moved to Palestine because they viewed it as their homeland and a safe haven for Jews, and as a result of the despair they felt for the future of the Jewish people — not on account of the instigation or urging of any colonial power or any other country;

c) the Zionists stood for the return of the Jewish people to their homeland, and there is no evidence that any colonial power ever initiated an effort to replace Arab Palestinians with returning Jews;

d) the Zionist movement did not contemplate territorial conquest and did not have an army that could have occupied Palestinian land, so conquering Palestine through military means on behalf of a colonial power was "not in the cards" – the initial act of pulling together any military unit did not occur until the Haganah's creation as a self-defense force was initiated in 1920, and although it can certainly be said that Israel won its War of Independence at least to some extent through the deployment of military forces following the invasion by five Arab armies in May 1948, the 1948 war was fought as a matter of that new nation's survival, not as an attempt at conquest by Israel;

e)   one would think that if the Jews who came to Palestine
were colonialists of any stripe, they would have emigrated from a motherland under whose sponsorship or
approval they were acting, but the fact is they arrived
in the largest numbers from Czarist Russia, Poland, and
other Eastern European countries that oppressed their
Jewish populations, and from Nazi Germany – applying
the phrase "colonialism" to a situation where a people
sought refuge from religious persecution by emigrating
to what they considered to be their ancestral homeland
gives a new meaning to "colonialism," which is defined
as a system or policy by which a country maintains foreign colonies, especially to exploit them economically;

f)   the British Government issued a White Paper in 1939
which limited the number of Jews who could enter Palestine to only 75,000 from 1939-44, thereby slamming
the door on Jewish immigration to Palestine precisely
when the Nazis were most intensely engaged in the
genocide of the Jewish people, and Jewish immigration
to Palestine was kept to zero during the three following
years – the British efforts to restrict Jewish immigration
were indeed a function of an attempt to appease the
Arabs and reduce the level of violence perpetrated
against the Jews, but limiting the entry of Jews was an
illogical step to initiate if Great Britain was intent on
acting as a colonizer of Palestine by using the Jews as a
tool to advance the colonization; and

g) the Jews, out of frustration and anger when the British began denying entry of Jews into Palestine, waged an armed struggle in Palestine against Great Britain, starting in the late 1930's and lasting until British troops left Palestine in 1947 — that heated conflict was responsible, in at least some measure, for helping to drive the British Empire from the Middle East and hastening the demise of colonialism in that part of the world.

The argument that Israel has colonialist underpinnings due to its linkage with the British mandate is without merit. Merely because Great Britain was given the mandate for Palestine in 1920 by a resolution signed at San Remo by the principal Allied powers involved in World War I is not in and of itself evidence that it was exercising colonial designs on Palestine. On the other hand, it is well-understood that a number of the countries that compose today's Arab world obtained nationhood following the Ottoman Empire's defeat in 1917 solely through the intervention, initiatives, and dictates of the European powers. It is ironic that the Arab world accepted, without raising the slightest fuss, the establishment by fiat issued by European powers of several nations in the Middle East with Muslim majorities, but rejected out-of-hand the mere concept of the creation of a single Jewish country. This acceptance is a critical point. If the continual Arab rejection of the presence of a Jewish state in the Middle East is founded in whole or part on the argument that Israel is a creature of colonialism, then why has the Arab world never challenged the legitimacy of Jordan, Syria, or Iraq, all of which were created by fiat?

Great Britain, at the time the world's greatest power, clearly embraced Zionism in 1917 with the issuance of the Balfour Declaration, the statement declaring Britain's support for a national home in Palestine for the Jewish people. Yet Britain never attempted during its mandate to grant Jews the right to govern a Jewish state. The reason was that it was the British view that such a right already existed on account of the historical connection between Palestine and the Jewish people. Recognition of those historical ties was the underlying basis for Britain supporting the creation of a Jewish homeland in Palestine. Yes, the British Empire changed the nature of all the societies it touched. There is no doubt that Britain's sphere of influence in the Middle East grew considerably during the 19th century. Any number of economic considerations caused British interest in the area to remain strong thereafter. But maintaining and strengthening economic ties to any country (or to the territory of Palestine) is a far cry from wielding power of the sort that produces a foreign colony that is exploited economically by the colonizer. There is nothing in the way of evidence to support the proposition that Britain intended to or did exploit the territory of Palestine economically. (One can make the likely presumption that no such evidence exists since there were no natural resources to be found in Palestine that a foreign country could possibly have considered exploitable.) What is key here is the firm evidence that Britain was acknowledging that the

Jews were deserving of a national home in Palestine due to the historical connection of the Jewish people with the land of Palestine, a position of the British that had nothing whatsoever to do with colonialism.

So I am hard-pressed to find any basis for the argument that the Palestinians are on solid ground in rejecting Israel's legitimacy and right to exist due to either Zionist colonialism or because Israel was a creation of a colonial power that sought to have Israel serve as an outpost of the colonizer. Rather, it is my view that the claims attempting to connect the Zionists or the State of Israel to colonialism represent nothing but an unfounded effort to undercut Israel's legitimacy and right to exist by making it appear as though the establishment of that nation would not have occurred but for some devious colonialist scheme "cooked up" by a colonial power either through its own devices or in collaboration with the Jews. Israel's rule over the land on which it sits has been challenged on numerous counts. But certainly, the charge of ties to colonialism appears to fail for lack of supportive evidence to at least as great an extent as any of the other accusations intended to undermine Israel's legitimacy and right to exist. Therefore, the charge of "colonialism" accomplishes nothing in attempting to undermine the premise that Israel's creation was justifiable and just.

This is as appropriate a time as any to make the point that for someone to reject the legitimacy and existence of Israel, no matter whether the rejection relies on the "colonialism" argument or any of the other rationales employed for denying Israel's legitimacy and right to exist, that person must disregard the historical association between the land of Palestine and the Jewish people. However, in a subsequent chapter, which deals with the matter of indigenous people, I will explain why those historical links between the Jews and Palestine simply cannot be erased or ignored as part of any strategy to delegitimize the State of Israel.

CHAPTER 9:

The Palestinian Refugees – Were They Displaced by the Zionists? Was Ethinic Cleansing Employed?

According to the Palestinian narrative, those Palestinians who are today referred to as the "Palestinian refugees" were forced from their homes, and their communities, by the Jews starting with the uptick in violence in December 1947 (violence instituted by the Palestinians to undermine the impact of the approval by the UN of its partition plan), and continuing during Israel's War of Independence. That war commenced on May 15, 1948, when the armies of five Arab countries (Egypt, Iraq, Jordan, Lebanon, and Syria, joined by volunteers from Morocco, Saudi Arabia, and Yemen) invaded Israel immediately following the proclamation of the state's birth with the widely announced goal of annihilating the new nation, and lasted until February 1949. Of course, if the Arab armies had not invaded Israel, no refugee problem would have arisen. Nonetheless, most Palestinians ignore that inconvenient but basic fact, and advance the argument that Israeli forces were solely responsible for the flight from their homes of the Palestinians who became refugees. A few proponents of the Palestinian narrative are willing to acknowledge that the acts of Palestinians and Arab countries may have been a secondary factor, but go on to declare that the refugee flow was primarily precipitated by the aggressive actions of the Israeli forces. However, whichever version of the Palestinian narrative on the refugee issue is offered, the intent of the charge that the Jews expelled Arabs is twofold. First, it is to rationalize continuing violence against Israel on the theory that if the Jews forcibly drove from their homes those who became refugees, the Palestinians are entitled to use force to regain their property. Second, it offers yet another pretext for why the Palestinians continue to reject Israel's legitimacy and right to exist. I hasten to raise the question, which is intended to be rhetorical, that if it is the right of the Palestinians to use force against the Jews of Israel to regain their property from which they were allegedly expelled, what is one to make of all the Arab violence against Jews in Palestine that occurred long before the refugee problem arose in 1948?

However phrased, the Palestinian narrative in this connection ignores the sad and ugly reality that all wars have consequences. And Israel's War of Independence was sure to have consequences, mainly because it derived from an invasion by five Arab armies intended to annihilate the Jews living in Israel and destroy the Jewish state just three years following the slaughter of millions of Jews in the Holocaust. One of the dismaying consequences of any war is the inevitable flow of refugees. So it was that approximately 750,000 Palestinians became refugees, first as a result of the five months of violence that preceded the War of Independence, and then as a consequence of the War of Independence itself (that number varies, depending on the source of the data, between the 600,000 claimed by some Israelis and the 900,000 claimed by some Palestinians, but historians most often cite the 750,000 figure).

The first order of business in discussing the refugee issue is to cover how Palestinians became refugees. Facts can prove stubborn, and here the facts tell the story of how the Arab world played a pivotal role in creating the massive number of Palestinian refugees and then causing them to linger in squalid refugee camps since 1948 solely to satisfy the political urges of Arab leaders and to serve the propaganda needs of the Arab world. The earliest phase of the refugee flow was not provoked by the actions of either the Palestinian Arabs or other Arabs, and certainly not by the Jews, but rather by the fear that a full-scale war was imminent. There is a great deal of information revealing that many Palestinians left their homes of their own accord even before the UN partition plan's approval, and then in the days following the rejection by the Palestinians of the partition plan approved by the UN on November 29,1947. These refugees sought safety in neighboring Arab countries from the anticipated war, expecting that they would return to Palestine when that war ended. There are no precise figures, or even well-founded estimates, on how many Palestinians left during this initial phase of the refugee flow, but guesstimates range from 100,000 to 200,000.

As the wave of violence against the Jews that commenced in December 1947 intensified, more Palestinians fled, expecting to return to their homes when the fighting ceased. Some left to escape the escalating violence, others left at the urging of leaders of the Palestinian paramilitary forces who wanted the Palestinians out of harm's way as the Jews were attacked (the leader of those Palestinian paramilitary units was the same person who, when serving as the Grand Mufti of Jerusalem, had collaborated with the Nazis and was an active supporter of the Nazi genocide of the Jews), others abandoned their homes at the urging or upon the orders of Arab leaders or local Arab politicians. Still others fled due to rumors (spread in some instances by Jewish fighters for tactical reasons) that an army composed of Jews from outside the Middle East was about to enter Palestine or that there were Jewish armed forces in Palestine with a military capability that far exceeded what the Arabs thought existed.

There is also vast amounts of evidence reflecting the great majority of those Palestinians who became refugees once the full-scale War of Independence started May 15, 1948, fled their communities to escape the war zone or because they were ordered or urged to do so by other Arabs, and not on account of any acts of the Israelis. It is historical truth that large numbers of Arab residents of what had become the State of Israel were ordered out of their towns and villages by their local Palestinian politicians, or urged to flee their homes by Arab leaders promising that those who left would be able to return following a short conflict and an assured Arab victory, or driven from their homes by the Arab armies that had invaded Israel upon the founding of the state. There is substantial indisputable evidence, in the form of declassified British Archives documents, press reports, Arab documents, personal testimony of both Arabs and Jews, and other sources, supporting the conclusion that there was no systematic expulsion of Palestinian Arabs by those defending the newly established State of Israel. That is not to say that there were no Palestinians whatsoever displaced due to Israel's military actions. No one who understands what war is like could believe that no instances of that sort happened, especially taking into consideration that the invasion of Israel upon its declaration of statehood was one of genocidal intent. As an example of what may have occurred as the Jews were defending themselves against the threats of massacre and extermination, it is well-documented that from the onset of hostilities on May 15, 1948, an objective of the military campaign conducted by the invading Arab armies was to achieve the evacuation of residents of Arab towns and villages to convert those sites into military posts. Should anyone be surprised that Israeli forces would have expelled Palestinians found to be still residing in communities that were transformed into Arab military bases that the Israelis were aiming to conquer and destroy?

But there can be no doubt that what had the most significant impact on the surging Palestinian refugee numbers were the seemingly countless known instances of Arab-instigated flight, particularly from cities and other larger communities, propelled by the Arab press, public speeches, and non-stop radio broadcasts. For example, tens of thousands of Arabs were ordered by

Arab leaders to leave Haifa. Their Arab leaders forced out thousands of Arab residents of Tiberius. In Jaffa, Israel's largest Arab city, Arab leaders ordered thousands of residents to evacuate. Jerusalem's Arab residents were ordered out of Arab neighborhoods by Arab leaders. Similar scenarios played out in other Arab population centers. And thousands of Arabs fled cities, towns, and villages due to the propaganda spread by Arab leaders, both Palestinian and otherwise, especially false allegations that the Jewish fighters were committing atrocities such as rape, torture, and the killing of defenseless children and women. However one explains why the Palestinians fled, the common thread in the explanations is that the Jews/Israelis did not contribute to the Palestinian refugee problem (except in connection with a particular circumstance that will be noted below). Rather, it was the Arabs, by virtue of their very invasion of Israel, the urgings and orders of Arab leaders, the spread of anti-Jewish propaganda, and the flight of Arab residents from the violence in the expectation that they would return to their homes after the anticipated Arab victory, who were to blame for the flight of Palestinians, and their consequent refugee status. Following the War of Independence, numerous accounts appeared in the Arab press throughout the Middle East acknowledging that the flight of Palestinians was caused or precipitated by the Arab states and their leaders, the implication set out in many of the articles being that since the Arabs created the problem, they were responsible for fixing it.

I want to emphasize that no evidence was uncovered or produced that the Jews, either before or during the War of Independence, devised or implemented a plan calling for the systematic expulsion of Arabs. Nor is there any evidence of any political scheme to systematically expel Arabs. The great majority of the Arabs who fled did so, as previously explained, to escape the war zone or because Arab politicians and leaders urged or ordered them to do so. On the other hand, several hundred thousand Arabs did not take flight. Those Arabs remaining in Israel were not harmed and they, and their descendants, became full Israeli citizens. This prompts me to return to the topic of ethnic cleansing. Now is the moment to confront the charge that the Palestinians' refusal to accept the legitimacy and right to exist of the State of Israel is warranted because the Jews committed ethnic cleansing of the Palestinian Arabs in the months preceding and during the War of Independence. The truth is that the Jews did not encourage Arabs who stayed behind to follow in the footsteps of their fellow Arabs who were leaving or had already fled. Not only that, but there are many well-documented instances of Jews having pleaded with Arab residents to stay. Plus, as noted, several hundred thousand Arabs chose to remain in place and were not discouraged by the Jews/Israelis from doing so. And how does one account for the fact that there are close to two million Arabs residing in Israel today (none of whom appear interested in fleeing Israel) if the Jews had engaged in ethnic cleansing? In short, the charge of ethnic cleansing seems to represent yet another of the spurious accusations asserted against the Jews by Palestinians to rationalize the refusal to accept Israel's legitimacy and existence. It does nothing to sour the argument that the establishment of Israel was justifiable and just.

Speaking of ethnic cleansing, I want to refer to several examples of authentic ethnic cleansing to drive home the point that the Jews did not engage in the ethnic cleansing of the Palestinian Arabs. For example, during the War of Independence, the Arab armies that had invaded Israel forcibly removed every last Jew from any and every area they captured, to say nothing of the fact that the Arabs systematically destroyed every synagogue and Jewish cemetery in Jerusalem while they controlled that city from 1948 until the "six-day war" in 1967. That was ethnic cleansing! As another example, following the proclamation of the birth of the State of Israel on May 14, 1948, Jewish life in virtually all Arab lands became intolerable due to anti-Jewish riots, the destruction of synagogues, newly-enacted exclusionary laws, and anti-Semitic propaganda. The result? Roughly 850,000 Jews were forced to flee and abandon their homes and other assets in Iraq, Algeria, Egypt, Yemen, Syria, Morocco, Lebanon, etc., thus becoming refugees like the 750,000 or so Palestinians who became refugees at the time of the founding of Israel. Today only a few thousand Jews remain in Arab countries. The flight of those Jews from Arab lands was due to ethnic cleansing! By the way, most of the Jewish refugees were absorbed by Israel (the rest by other countries), unlike the Palestinian refugees and their descendants who have purposely been required to remain in refugee camps ever since 1948 for purely political reasons, i.e., in order to maintain their refugee status as a weapon against Israel. Palestinian leaders and Arab states have prevented the refugees from resettling and resuming normal lives in any Arab country with the exception of Jordan, where Palestinian refugees have been granted citizenship.

In addition to the reasons already set out above in support of the argument that the Jews did not systematically expel Arabs from Palestine either before or during the War of Independence, there is another compelling circumstance that reinforces that position. Exhaustive studies were conducted of the coverage by several independent news sources (the Chicago Tribune, Associated Press, and United Press International) of Palestine and the Middle East between January 1947 and December 1949. Each of those news sources had reporters assigned to cover events in Palestine personally. Yet the investigation did not uncover even one report published during that three year period that mentioned the Jews expelling or having expelled Arabs from Palestine/Israel. And news reports appearing in newspapers throughout the world about the situation in Israel as the War of Independence progressed, including those in publications that relied on dispatches from their reporters stationed in Israel, were devoid of references to the Israeli army expelling Arabs. It was only after the "six-day war" in 1967 that the plight of the displaced Palestinians began to appear in accounts of the history of the conflict between the Jews and Arabs to elicit sympathy for the Palestinian cause.

It also needs to be noted that following the end of the War of Independence in February 1949, and for five decades after that, Israeli Jews continually visited, shopped, and ate in Arab towns and villages in Israel without a second thought. They freely socialized with Arabs in those communities. Unfortunately, that all started to unravel with the outbreak of Palestinian terror in 2000. The inherent risks to Jewish lives caused by that terrorism brought to an end the tranquil days when Jews and Arabs mixed together freely in Israel (and even in the occupied West Bank). I do not believe that the sort of business and social contacts between Arabs and Jews that occurred in Israel for 50 years before 2000 would have been possible had the Palestinian Arab population believed even for a second that hundreds of thousands of fellow Arabs were forced to abandon their homes by the Jews in 1948.

There are two additional points I would like to make concerning the "refugees." The first is that many of the Arabs who fled in 1948 were relative newcomers to the territory of Palestine, having arrived in the 1920's, 30's, and 40's from various Arab countries to take advantage of the economic prosperity that the Zionists had generated. To place such relatively recent arrivals to Palestine who then became refugees (and about whom it could be said that they had their roots not in Palestine, but in the countries where they lived before moving to Palestine) in the same category as those who fled and whose roots in the land of Palestine went back centuries, is arguably quite a stretch. However, I have no interest in quibbling over the detail of how to establish who among the refugees deserved to be categorized as "real" or "true" Palestinians. Also, as alluded to in a prior chapter, a large proportion of those Arabs who had genuine roots in Palestine and fled in 1948 did not own the property they left behind. They were tenant farmers on land that had been acquired largely by absentee Arab landlords according to laws enacted by the Ottoman Empire in the mid-19th century. I have chosen not to pursue in any respect the issue of who held legal ownership of the property that was abandoned by fleeing Palestinians, since it seems to me that the identity of the legal owner does not matter for present purposes.

Let's now address Palestinian claims that some individuals or groups fighting to defend Israel and its Jewish citizens forced Palestinians to flee. Those claims center around events in the city of Lydda from July 11-13, 1948. A brief bit of background is in order. Almost immediately following David Ben-Gurion's declaration of Israel's independence on May 14, 1948, five Arab armies invaded the newly-born country. The Jordanian Arab Legion laid siege to Jerusalem. Israeli military leaders concluded that military necessity then required that Israeli forces conquer a number of Arab towns and villages to protect the heartland of Israel, the area between Jerusalem and Tel Aviv. In particular, the Israelis determined that to remove the threat to Tel Aviv (Israel's largest city) and to save Jerusalem's Jews from annihilation, they needed to secure the road running from Jerusalem to Tel Aviv (the only road between the two cities), which the Jordanians had already come close to severing. Lydda was situated eleven miles from Tel Aviv along the road stretching from Jerusalem to Tel Aviv. And so it was that the newly formed Israel Defense Forces expelled some 35,000 Arabs from Lydda, as well as much smaller numbers of Arabs from some of the villages that also straddled the key road between Jerusalem and Tel Aviv.

However, the expulsion of the Arabs by the Israeli army from Lydda and other smaller Arab communities lining the Tel Aviv-Jerusalem road must be examined in the context of military strategy. Israel's urgent military objective at the time was to secure the road for critical tactical reasons. The new state was engaged in defending itself in a war launched by the Arab states for the very express purpose of annihilating the Jews of Israel. The goal of annihilation, as distinguished from an undertaking to recover land previously lost in battle, was enunciated repeatedly in the public rhetoric of the leaders of the Arab states. A failure to act forcefully and decisively in Israel's strategic interests could have meant that the Jews would quickly and brutally be driven into the Mediterranean Sea, which was the Arab invaders' oft-stated goal. It would not be unreasonable in my view to argue that just as the Palestinian refugee problem was a result born of a war started by the Arabs, so too was the expulsion of Arabs from Lydda a consequence of a war started by the Arabs. But more precisely, the removal of Arabs from Lydda and villages along the Jerusalem-Tel Aviv highway by Israeli forces was a purely tactical military measure dictated entirely by military considerations. Yes, those particular Arabs, relatively small in number compared to the hundreds of thousands who fled Palestine/Israel through no fault or intention of the Jews, were expelled from their homes by the Israelis and became refugees. But there is no equivalency of any sort between the expulsion, for tactical military reasons by Israeli armed forces, of Arabs living along the Jerusalem-Tel Aviv corridor, and the flight of all the other Arabs who abandoned their homes and also became refugees.

Having referred to the expulsion of Arabs from Lydda by Israeli forces, what happened at the village of Deir Yassin must also be touched upon. Deir Yassin, situated near Jerusalem and overlooking the Jerusalem-Tel Aviv road that the Jews viewed as a lifeline to the Jews of Jerusalem, was attacked by a contingent of the Irgun (a splinter group not directly attached to the Haganah) on April 9, 1948. The Irgun force sought to remove a unit of Iraqi soldiers who had entered the village about a month earlier. The Iraqis' presence made the village fair game for the Irgun operation, especially due to fear that the Iraqis would attempt to disrupt access for Jews to the Jerusalem-Tel Aviv road. During the ensuing battle for control of the village, which ultimately ended with the capture or killing of the Iraqi soldiers, numerous innocent women and other civilians were killed by Irgun gunfire. The Irgun was accused by the Arabs of having perpetrated a massacre, and Arab propaganda generated subsequent to the fighting falsely accused the Jews of murdering an exaggerated number of Arabs, and committing every sort of imaginable (and unimaginable) atrocity upon the citizens of Deir Yassin. Following the battle in Deir Yassin, Palestinians throughout the territory were warned by Arab leaders that the Jews would kill them if they did not flee their homes, citing the purported Deir Yassin "massacre" as an example of what would happen to them. There is no question that the propaganda spewed by the Arabs about the battle at Deir Yassin contributed to the flight of many thousands of Palestinians from their homes across Palestine in the months leading up to the War of Independence.

But upon further examination of the facts, one can conclude that no massacre occurred at Deir Yassin. The Red Cross, which was involved in treating the wounded, found no evidence that a massacre had taken place. Likewise, Arab investigators who reviewed the evidence found that civilians who died were caught in vicious crossfire (the total number of Arab deaths, including Iraqi soldiers, was calculated by Arab investigators at 107). Based on interviews with civilian survivors of the Deir Yassin battle, it appears beyond dispute that the lies contained in the Arab propaganda, and especially the false reports of atrocities committed by the Irgun, were formulated to encourage the Arab countries to enter the conflict being waged at that point in time by tens of thousands of Palestinian Arabs serving in paramilitary units. I must stress that even though Arab propaganda, past and present, charges that Deir Yassin was but one of many instances of massacres for which the Jews were responsible, the Arabs have never documented any similar alleged massacres committed by the Jews during the War of Independence or the months preceding that war.

Concerning the tendency of the Palestinians to allege with some regularity the commission since 1948 of massacres of innocent Palestinians by Israeli military forces, a charge that is asserted in defense of the rejection by Palestinians of the legitimacy and existence of Israel, I must cite what happened in April 2002 in the West Bank city of Jenin. Headlines around the world screamed out for days that, based on "eyewitness" accounts and other reports received from Palestinian sources, the Israel Defense Forces had slaughtered many hundreds of people during a counter-terrorist operation carried out in Jenin. It turns out that 54 bodies of Palestinians were found in Jenin, a number eventually confirmed by Palestinian officials, who also acknowledged that most of the dead were armed members of terrorist groups. Old Palestinian habits, such as inventing massacres that never happened — allegedly committed by Jews — die hard.

We cannot conclude this discussion about the Palestinian refugees without examining the question of whether there is an actual "refugee" problem today concerning the Palestinians who fled Palestine between November 29, 1947, when the UN partition plan was approved, and February 1949, when a cease-fire brought the War of Independence to an end. Commonly, a refugee is defined as a person who flees a country due to war or political or religious persecution and seeks refuge elsewhere. However, a Palestinian refugee is an individual who fled Palestine/Israel — plus all persons who are descendants of the person who fled. Putting aside for the moment the issue of how or why Palestinians became refugees between November 1947 and January 1949, the current estimates are that only 20,000 or so of the actual 1948 refugees are still alive to claim refugee status under the standard definition of "refugee." The expanded definition of "refugee" to include "descendants," which was adopted by the United Nations Relief and Works Administration (UNRWA), a special UN agency established to deal solely with Palestinians, means that there are today more than 5,000,000 children, grandchildren, and great-grandchildren of the 1948 refugees (possibly as many as 7,000,000 according to some estimates) who are now claiming refugee status. And that number, whatever it is exactly, keeps growing. Only Palestinian refugees have ever been defined to include descendants. I also hasten to note that of all the refugee issues that arose during the 20th century, including those created by World Wars I and II, only that involving the Palestinian Arabs remains to be resolved. I will leave it to others to debate whether UNRWA has been complicit in the effort to ensure that the Palestinian "refugees," who continue to be a substantial financial burden on the whole world, remain a weapon in the Palestinians' anti-Israel arsenal.

Undoubtedly, the 20,000 or so still-living original refugees could be repatriated to Israel if the Palestinians were interested in negotiating the details. Furthermore, suppose peace was truly the goal of the Palestinians. In that case, the Arab countries could in short order integrate the descendants of the original refugees into their societies, just as Israel did with Jewish refugees from Arab countries. However, the 5,000,000 or more remain confined to refugee camps to promote the Palestinians' anti-Israel narrative, which encourages generation after generation of "refugees" to consider themselves helpless victims of evil Israel and feeds them detestable anti-Jewish rhetoric. The "refugees" are used as pawns in the strategy employed by the Palestinians to put an end to the sovereign State of Israel by insisting upon the "right of return" for every Palestinian "refugee." Israel argues, in my judgment with great merit, that the demand that the still-living original refugees and all their descendants be allowed to return is yet another example of Palestinian rejection of the legitimacy of the Jewish state in what is the ancestral homeland of the Jews, as well as of Israel's right to exist. Such a return of Palestinians would threaten to turn Israel into an Arab state due to the enormous demographic shift that would occur. That eventuality would clearly be the death knell of Israel. The Palestinians understand perfectly well that the influx of these refugees, even assuming some would prefer not returning to Israel, would signal the end of the democratic Jewish state. And lest anyone challenge the desire of Israel to maintain its identity as a Jewish state, please do not lose sight of the fact that Islam is the official religion in virtually every Arab country on this earth, as well as in some non-Arab states. It is pure hypocrisy of the basest sort to oppose the right of the Jewish people to express their national home in terms of it being a Jewish state but not raise any objection to the existence of the world's Islamic states (or of Christian states).

There can certainly be a valid criticism of some of the actions and policies of Israel. Still, I am quite frustrated and annoyed that Israel is continually required to justify its legitimacy and right to exist when confronted with the charge that Palestinian refugees have suffered severe hardships as a result of the Jewish state's creation. It is critical to this discussion to keep in mind that if the Palestinians had accepted the UN partition plan, there would have been no War of Independence, no Palestinian refugees, and two states with Arabs living as neighbors of Jews. While serving as Israel's Ambassador to the UN, Abba Eban stated on November 17, 1958, "The Arab refugee problem was caused by a war of aggression, launched by the Arab states against Israel in 1947 and 1948. Let there be no mistake. If there had been no war against Israel . . . there would be no problem of Arab refugees today. Once you determine the responsibility for that war, you have determined the responsibility for the refugee problem." And as has been described in this chapter, there are plenty of other well-documented explanations for why the Jews should not be held culpable for creating the Palestinian refugee problem. As it is, Israel in the past has indicated a willingness to contribute substantially to a compensation package that would be extended to the refugees, including descendants, intended to help underwrite resettlement costs. Still, of course, refugee resettlement is not on the Palestinian radar screen because resettlement would result in the evaporation of the prospect that Israel someday could be forced to accept so many refugees that it would lose its Jewish character. Everything considered, it is tough to understand how any fair-minded observer could or would possibly conclude that the existence of those "refugees" diminishes the strength of the position that Israel's establishment was justifiable and just. But that's the reader's call.

If it occurred to you that the invasion of the new State of Israel on May 15, 1948, involved the armies of five Arab countries and volunteers from at least three other Arab nations, but that the Palestinians themselves did not participate in the invasion, you are technically correct. However, this circumstance should not, and does not, absolve the Palestinians from full responsibility for the events that marked and flowed from Israel's War of Independence, particularly the creation of the Palestinian refugee problem. The Palestinians had rejected the UN partition plan, and then initiated violent armed attacks upon the

Jews in Palestine by tens of thousands of members of Palestinian paramilitary forces. Those clashes continued until the day of the invasion, causing the loss of close to 2,000 Jewish lives. The Palestinians then actively supported, both as battlefield participants and otherwise in every respect, the invading armies. Let's call the Palestinian role in the invasion what it was, namely full participation in the military engagement other than the absence of Palestinian soldiers actually crossing Israel's borders with the invading Arab armies. The mere fact that Palestinian forces did not participate logistically in the incursion across Israel's borders by the Arab armies does not relieve the Palestinians of any of the blame for the refugee problem.

CHAPTER 10:

A Key Question: Are Jewish People Indigenous to the Land of Palestine?

Numerous prior pages of this book have contained mention of the Jewish people's historical connection to the land of Palestine. Citing this link between the Jews and their ancestral home, often referred to in terms of a continuous Jewish presence in Palestine for 3,000 years, inevitably leads to a consideration of the issue of whether Palestinians or Jews, or both, are indigenous to the land of Palestine. This is a critical issue because it is a principle of international law that indigenous people have the right to possess any territory and accompanying natural resources that they traditionally owned or in which they naturally originated. But to be an indigenous people to particular land, there must be a continuous identity stretching back to the relevant historical period of that land. If the case can be made that Jews are indigenous to Palestine, then it would follow as clearly as day follows night and night follows day that there is enormous merit to the argument that the establishment of the State of Israel in 1948 was justifiable and just. That is why Palestinian Arabs, to rationalize their rejection of Israel's legitimacy and existence, have been attempting to turn history on its head by denying the historical Jewish connection to the land of Palestine.

Let's first cite some of the outlandish ways in which the Palestinians have sought to toss cold water on the Jewish people's claim that they are indigenous to the land of Palestine. In their frenzied attempts to completely nullify the link of the Jewish people to their ancient homeland, and to in effect erase Jews from the history of the Holy Land, the Palestinian Arabs have embraced a warped narrative that advances such notions as (a) Jesus was a Palestinian (probably historically impossible, but in any event the common consensus among historians and researchers is that he was a Jew), (b) the "Palestinians" are "the indigenous people" of Palestine (see the discussion later in this chapter that argues to the contrary), (c) Jews are squatters on the land the Palestinians have owned for 5,000 years (keep in mind that the Muslim Arab conquest of Palestine did not occur until the fourth decade of the 7th century, a fact that obviously places in serious question the Palestinian claim of ownership for 5,000 years), (d) there is no evidence of Jewish life in Palestine prior to 1948 (Huh?), (e) the Jews were not part of the Palestinian population until they arrived as invaders in 1948 (Huh?), (f) the Jews have no historical connections to Jerusalem (Huh?), (g) the Jews have no historical connections to Jerusalem's holy sites, having invented the story about a Temple once having been situated on the Temple Mount (the First Temple was built during the 10th century B.C.E. and destroyed in 586 B.C.E., the Second Temple was completed in 515 B.C.E. and stood until destroyed by the Romans in 70 C.E. — numerous historical sources have recorded that they personally observed, depending when the observation occurred, either the First or Second Jewish Temple standing on the Temple Mount), (h) the Western Wall has no connection to Judaism (this preposterous claim appeared in a report issued by the Palestinian Authority in December 2010, a report that it was forced to retract following an international outcry — Jews have worshipped at the foot of the Western Wall, a surviving remnant of the Temple Mount where the two Temples stood, since the destruction of Jerusalem and the Second Temple in 70 C.E., (i) the Western Wall belongs only to Muslims (Huh?), (j) the Palestinians are descended from the Canaanites, who resided in Palestine 5,000 years ago (this claim does not appear to have any basis in fact or history, but nonetheless raises the question of how the Palestinians can possibly be Arabs if they were Canaanites, inasmuch as the Arabs came to the land of Palestine in the fourth decade of the 7th century from the Arabian Peninsula?), and (k) Israel forges and otherwise changes archeological finds and writes on them in Hebrew (there has never been any evidence offered by the Palestinians to support this type of allegation). These sorts of mistruths, which are aimed at refuting the longstanding historical ties of the Jews to Palestine, are rooted in the need of the Palestinians to argue that the country of Israel is stolen Arab land, which then justifies, in their view, their rejection of modern Israel's legitimacy and right to exist. Applying the term "mistruths" is supported by the circumstance that there has been no documentation forthcoming from the Palestinians of such claims as those I have just enumerated.

At the risk of belaboring the issue, I want to discuss further the claim noted as item (j) above related to the Palestinians purportedly being descended from the Canaanites, who resided in Palestine 5,000 years ago. The Palestinian leadership has been repeatedly repeating this claim of late for the rather obvious reason that the Canaanites were in Palestine before the Israelite tribes. But this alleged link to the Canaanites falls flat on its face when one considers that there is no evidence that any Palestinian families or tribes refer to a Canaanite origin. They see themselves as Arabs descended from Arab tribes. I guess the best way of summing up this relatively recent addendum to the Palestinian narrative is to suggest that just because a Palestinian leader says something about Palestinian history does not make it so.

The Palestinians have doggedly maintained and successfully sustained their twisted narrative over the recent decades. As best I can figure out, that narrative survives through some combination of anti-Jewish bigotry, a lack of interest in learning the details of Middle Eastern history, ignorance of Jewish history, indifference to world affairs, a reluctance to take sides, the propensity of people to imagine there must be some degree of truth to information that is conveyed relentlessly in the unending campaign to elicit sympathy for the Palestinian cause, and the phenomenon that if enough of something is thrown against a wall, some of it is bound to stick. Unfortunately, it has not been possible to halt the narrative voiced by Palestinian leaders which has been promoted even by so-called moderate Palestinians, that Palestine was not the ancient homeland of the Jewish people. All one can do is rebut the mistruths, which ultimately leads to the inconvenient truth for the Palestinian Arabs that there has been a continuous Jewish presence in the historical land of Palestine for something in the vicinity of 3,000 years. No matter how creative the Palestinian approach to history, the evidence proves that Jews are indigenous to the Holy Land, which means that, as indigenous people, they have the right to possess the land (or at least a portion of the territory) that they previously inhabited, in this case, the land of Palestine. Most of the mistruths put forward by the Palestinian narrative can be disproved by visiting one of the many archeological sites that have been excavated in the land that was Palestine. But let's examine the facts that are ignored by those who push the Palestinian narrative that seeks to erase the Jewish connection to the land of Palestine, which is tied to the effort to deny Israel's legitimacy and right to exist. Where to begin?

Probably the best place to start is to emphasize that for almost 1,900 years since the exile of the Jews following the destruction by the Romans of Jerusalem and the Second Temple in 70 C.E., there has been a continuous presence of Jewish residents in the land of Palestine (a reference to pertinent historical facts that predate 70 C.E. will appear elsewhere in this chapter). That constant presence is underscored by the fact that some of the Jews living in Palestine at the time of the Second Temple's destruction remained in their communities in Palestine rather than going into exile. Also, pious Jews made their way to Palestine from all parts of the world throughout the centuries of exile, many to reside there and others to live out the final years of their lives and then to be buried in the sacred soil of the Holy Land. Jews lived continuously in Palestine after 70 C.E. under Byzantine, Muslim, and Crusader rule. The evidence is clear that until the 5th century C.E., Jews represented a significant portion (but certainly less than a majority) of the population in the Galileé, a northern region of the territory of Palestine, and during that period, Jewish life thrived in the city of Tiberius. It is well-established that Jews resided in Palestine at the time of the Muslim Arab conquest in the fourth decade of the 7th century. A 9th century map shows scores of Jewish communities in Palestine, of which we have archeological evidence today. Accounts of the Crusader conquest of Jerusalem in 1099 refer to Jews as stalwart defenders of the land, fighting and dying during the resistance to Crusader rule. During the period between the defeat of the Crusaders and 1517, when the Ottoman Empire commenced its 400-year rule of Palestine, the city of Acre became populated by Jews, and records reveal the presence of nearly thirty Jewish communities at the beginning of the 16th century. Following the expulsion of Jews from Spain and Portugal in the late 15th century and their arrival in the Holy Land, Safed became the largest Jewish community in Palestine and a center for Jewish studies. When the Ottoman conquest happened in 1517, Jews lived in Jerusalem, Nablus, Hebron, Safed, and in villages in the Galilee. Ottoman tax registers dating from the 16th century reveal the names of Jewish taxpayers residing in Palestine, including those of rabbis. Jews came to Palestine from Eastern Europe in the late 18th and early 19th centuries to live, particularly in Jerusalem, Safed, Tiberius, and Hebron. By the mid-19th century, nearly a half-century before the Zionist movement's founding, Jews had become the largest religious community in Jerusalem. In 1906, eleven years before the Balfour Declaration, Jerusalem's total population was estimated to have been 60,000, of whom 7,000 were Muslims, 13,000 were Christians, and 40,000 were Jews.

At the beginning of the 20th century, the number of Jews in the land that became Israel was about 80,000. This represented at best roughly 50 percent of the number of Arabs populating that area (if one includes what is today the West Bank and Gaza, the total population of Palestine is believed to have been roughly 500,000 in the early 1880's). However, whether people are indigenous to a land is not dependent on whether their group constantly remains predominant in terms of population in its ancestral homeland. And the abundant facts just described, as well as additional evidence that will be covered shortly, reveal that there has always been a Jewish presence in the area commonly referred to as Palestine. This continuous presence is arguably by itself all the evidence one requires to prevail on the issue of whether Jews are indigenous to the land that became Israel in 1948. If the Jews are indigenous, it follows that the Jews are entitled to possess the territory (or at least a portion thereof) in which their people traditionally resided, meaning that the establishment of the modern State of Israel was justifiable and just. Jews who moved to what is now Israel beginning in the early 1880's, as well as the Zionists who subsequently came in larger numbers, had the same clear right to do so as had the Jews who came to reside in their ancient homeland over the prior centuries. They were seeking to begin new lives in peace and free of discrimination in a place their ancestors had long ago settled, and where there had always been a known and well-documented continuous Jewish presence.

It is interesting that while Jewish life in the land of Palestine persisted during nineteen centuries of exile of most Jews from that land following the Roman destruction of Jerusalem and the Second Temple in 70 C.E., never during those 1,900 years did any other people lay claim to the land of Palestine as their country, nor did any other people undertake the effort of building the land into a nation or even take elementary steps that could have placed the Palestinians on the road to statehood. Beginning in the first decade of the 20th century, the Jewish community in Palestine started organizing itself so that it could eventually self-govern. Only after the Zionists "made their move" by initiating the Zionist movement at the very end of the 19th century, and then began to establish the attributes of a state in Palestine, did the Palestinian Arabs first claim the land as theirs.

Now, let's take a look at the archeological evidence supporting the fact of the Jewish people's enduring presence in the land of Palestine going back thousands of years. Today's Israel contains the greatest density of archeological sites of any country in the world. Archeologists are continually recovering artifacts that testify scientifically to ancient Jewish life in Palestine.

The archeological proof of the Jewish connection to the land of Palestine is indisputable and overwhelming. For example, the ruins of numerous ancient synagogues have been uncovered. The oldest synagogue yet discovered dates back to 75 B.C.E. What more solid factual evidence than the ancient synagogues that have been excavated is necessary to prove that the land of Palestine is the birthplace of Jewish history, thus making Jewish people indigenous to that land?

There is much more archeological evidence to describe. The ancient biblical manuscripts, known as the Dead Sea Scrolls, are generally agreed to date from the 1st century B.C.E. based on the Hebrew script and on archeological data. A scroll with the Priestly Benediction, believed to date back to the 7th century B.C.E., is among the oldest of the Hebrew biblical texts found. Artifacts retrieved from soil in the vicinity of the Temple Mount in Jerusalem include, for example, a Greek inscription warning non-Jews not to enter further into the Temple compound, a clay seal used by the Temple priests to keep track of commerce related to sacrificial offerings, and over 800 Jewish coins from the Second Temple period. Additionally, numerous Jewish ritual purification baths have been found in the area surrounding the Temple Mount. Many artifacts have been discovered by archeologists containing ancient Hebrew script on them, proving an ancient Jewish presence all across the land of Palestine. The inscriptions appear on pottery. They are carved on walls. They number in the thousands, and they have been uncovered in hundreds of excavated locations, both urban and rural, including caves and burial tombs. I note again that the inscriptions are in the Hebrew language, which is known to have been the language of the Jewish people going back 3,000 years, and the texts can be accurately dated by biblical scholars by studying the changes in the Hebrew scripts on the inscriptions. Scores of foreign inscriptions have also been found, the contents of which make it clear that people from neighboring lands knew that Israelites inhabited the land of Palestine. Please be aware that no Palestinian Arab archeological findings have ever been discovered that serve as evidence of historical Palestinian Arab links to the land of Palestine.

Let me throw in one more piece of archeological evidence just for good measure. This summer (of 2020), while I was writing this book, a large accumulation of royal Kingdom of Judah seal impressions was uncovered at a First Temple-period public tax collection and storage complex excavated about two miles from Jerusalem's Old City. Archeologists believe that the complex served as an administrative center during the 8th and 7th centuries B.C.E. Over 120 jar handles stamped roughly 2,700 years ago with ancient Hebrew script seal impressions were discovered.

Non-Jews have spoken about the historical connection between the Jewish people and the Holy Land. Ever since the Muslim Arabs conquered Palestine almost 1,400 years ago, a long list of prominent Muslim religious figures have written about the Temple Mount as the location of the Second Jewish Temple. Arabs themselves have acknowledged that Jews are indigenous to the land of Palestine, several Arabs having done so in writings published in the first two decades of the 20th century in which they welcomed the Jews back to their homeland. The Koran itself is explicit about the Jewish people's destiny, reciting that the Holy Land is designated for the followers of Moses, and nowhere does the Koran assert or even touch upon any justification for a claim to Palestine by persons of the Muslim faith. And let's not forget the declaration of the Romans, following the destruction of Jerusalem and the Second Temple in 70 C.E., that the land of Israel would be no more.

Jewish religious practice serves as a strong indicator of the historical connection of the Jews to the land of Palestine. The Jewish people have prayed daily for 2,000 years for their return to the Jewish homeland. Jews everywhere have faced in the direction of Jerusalem when praying over the past 2,000 years. During the Seder, the meal that takes place on the eve of the first day of the holiday of Passover, which commemorates the exodus of the Jews from Egypt, those participating in the Seder proclaim "Next year in Jerusalem." Jerusalem is central to the Jewish religion and Jewish prayer. On the other hand, Jerusalem is not mentioned even once in the Koran, nor is it cited in Muslim prayers. The religion of Islam has never expressed any interest in incorporating Jerusalem into the scheme of the Muslim faith. During the close to one thousand years of Muslim rule over Jerusalem that occurred in the period starting in the fourth decade of the 7th century and running through the Ottoman Empire's demise in 1917, the city never served as the capital of any part of the Muslim world. Although the Al-Aqsa Mosque on the Temple Mount is certainly significant in Islam, the city of Jerusalem has no religious meaning to Muslims (the

Al-Aqsa Mosque is the third holiest mosque in Islam, after mosques in Mecca and Medina).

Let's close the circle on whether Jews are indigenous to the land of Palestine by referring to the impact of international law on the question. As was discussed in an earlier chapter, the 1917 Balfour Declaration contained a legally binding commitment by Great Britain to support the creation of a Jewish homeland in Palestine based on the historical ties between the Jewish people and the land of Palestine. The San Remo Resolution in 1920 and the mandate for Palestine unanimously approved by the League of Nations in 1923 recognized and reinforced the indigenous rights of the Jewish people to their historical homeland. Their right to settle in their historic homeland and establish their state in the land of Palestine was and is a legal right anchored in international law. So, according to international law, Jews are indigenous people of the land of Palestine.

You will note that regarding the evidence I presented on the subject of whether Jewish people are indigenous to the land of Palestine, I have not to this point injected into the mix the oft-heard assertion that the Palestinian Arabs cannot possibly be indigenous to that land because Palestinian identity was not invented until the 1960's (around the time of the creation of the Palestinian Liberation Organization in 1964) as a political tactic in the struggle against Israel's establishment and to destroy the validity of the State of Israel. The name "Palestine" derives from the Romans. They affixed that name to the Holy Land either as an intended insult to the Jews for capitulating to the

Roman conquest of Jerusalem, or because the Romans wanted to erase Jewish links to the land (different sources provide divergent explanations, some stating that the reason for naming the land "Palestine" is unknown). However, no nation or political entity called Palestine was ever created, not even during the 400-year life of the Ottoman Empire. There has never been a state or country inhabited by "Palestinians." During the period of the British mandate, the people referred to as Palestinian were the Jews. The Arabs were referred to as Arabs, with no attempt at geographic distinction. Therefore, goes the argument that there has never been a state of Palestine, it was necessary to construct the image of a Palestinian state, because if there is no Palestinian state there can be no Palestinian people, and if there are no Palestinian people, who would be in a position to fight the battle to eliminate Israel's presence in what had been the territory of Palestine?

It is evident that no people could better argue that the Palestinians are the indigenous people of Palestine, and therefore the rightful owners of the land of Palestine, than Palestinians. First, however, the mother of historical fabrications had to be "cooked up," namely that there was long ago a state of Palestine and a Palestine people when in fact there has never been a state of Palestine and the Arabs living in the land of Palestine did not begin identifying themselves as Palestinians until well after modern Israel was established in 1948 (they previously had identified with Arab countries, most notably Syria). I could cite chapter and verse of the various arguments that have emerged, as an outgrowth of the position that a state of Palestine has never existed, that have been applied to negate the Palestinians' claim to be the rightful inheritors of the land of Palestine, but I have chosen not to further press that point. The reason for my not doing so is my view that even if one accepts that there is not now and has never been a Palestinian state, such a result has no bearing on the issue of whether the creation of Israel was justifiable and just (such a result does go to the narrower question of how Israel could possibly have been created out of Palestinian land if the concept of Palestine as a nation and Palestinians as a separate people did not gain some traction until after modern Israel was born in 1948?). What does count for a lot in determining whether the establishment of Israel in 1948 was justifiable and just is whether one can be accepting of the principle that the birth of modern Israel flowed from history's longest unbroken link of a people to a homeland where their ancestors practiced the same religion and spoke the same language roughly 3,000 years ago. It is a proposition that virtually every historian acknowledges, i.e., that Judaism, the Hebrew language, and the Jewish people were born in the Holy Land 3,000 years ago, and that Jews have had a continuous presence in the area that now includes Israel for all of those thirty or so centuries. On the other hand, the Arab presence did not occur until the Muslim Arab conquest of the territory of Palestine in the fourth decade of the 7th century. Yet the Palestinians remain unceasing in their campaign to belittle the links between the Jews and the land of Palestine, as thoroughly documented in a mass of historic and archeological records, and to deny Israel's legitimacy and right to exist.

You may have also noticed that I have not attempted to examine Jewish history based on the massive number of Biblical references to either people of the Jewish faith or to cities, towns, villages, or religious sites having Jewish significance. As even anyone who has little more than a passing familiarity with the Bible story is aware, those Biblical references (that appear in both the Old and New Testaments) establish that there is deep Jewish history in Palestine dating back to antiquity that predates Arab history in the Holy Land by more than two thousand years and that Jerusalem has been the focus and at the center of that history of the Jewish people for over 3,000 years. Just for some slight perspective, Jerusalem is named almost 700 times in the Bible, but not once in the Koran. As I have explained previously, it was the historical connection with the land of Palestine, which includes a multitude of ancient links cited in the Bible, that convinced the international community in the 20th century to support the creation of a Jewish homeland in Palestine. However, in the interest of avoiding protests that challenge what the Bible says on the basis that there is no way of knowing for certain that what is contained in the Bible is precisely accurate, I am not relying upon pertinent Biblical references to help support the case that Jews are indigenous to the land of Palestine. Having said that, it has been difficult to restrain myself from spelling out the details of the Jewish link to the Holy Land before the time of Christ, such as the key consideration that from 1004 to 587 B.C.E., or for more than 400 years, King David (who unified the Israelite tribes into a nation and made Jerusalem its capital) and his male heirs reigned in Jerusalem. However, I have exercised the necessary amount of self-control so as to withstand the temptation to open the flood-gates to relevant Biblical references.

But even without drawing upon the Bible's content, the array of evidence is vast in support of the argument that the Jewish people had their historical roots in the land of Palestine and, given their continuous presence there, are indigenous to that land. The argument does not rest on a few isolated archeological finds or upon a random historical event. Instead, it is founded upon a massive amount of archeological and historical evidence (leaving aside the "tons" of pertinent Biblical references) assembled by hundreds of archeologists and their thousands of crew members and by many renowned historians and competent researchers, all representing various religions and a multitude of countries.

I hope that you have grasped from a reading of this chapter that I have never once declared that the Jewish people are "the" indigenous people of the land of Palestine. I have not meant to even suggest that only the Jews could be deemed to be indigenous to that land. I have tried to present evidence that backs up the claim that Jews are indigenous to Palestine without dismissing the possibility that other people may also be indigenous to that territory. On the other hand, in light of all that I have recounted, and due secondarily to the fact that there is no reference in recorded history, at least not until the second half of the 20th century, to any Muslim or Arab people being called "Palestinian" or claiming to be "Palestinians," I am unable to establish any basis for concluding that the Palestinian Arabs are indigenous to the land of Palestine. However, I gladly agree that Arabs share the connection of the Jewish people with the Holy Land, and like the Jews, have a claim to the land of Palestine. But let me be as emphatic as I can be in asserting my belief that the Palestinian claim rests on the presence of Arabs in the land of Palestine since Islam's conquest of the Holy Land in the fourth decade of the 7th century, and not on any premise that the Palestinians were the original inhabitants of the Holy Land. The Arab people cannot become indigenous to the land merely by conquering an indigenous people of that land.

Also, one must consider, in connection with the Palestinian claim to the land of Palestine, that commencing at the end of the 19th century, but with the numbers surging after World War I, tens of thousands of Arabs from countries composing the Ottoman Empire migrated to the territory of Palestine to benefit from the growing economic prosperity of the region generated by the Zionists, which meant greater opportunities for Arabs to obtain work than were available in their homelands and to take advantage of Palestine's rising living standards. The Arab population grew by 1947 to approximately 1.2 million in what was mandatory Palestine (by the way, Yasser Arafat, who was born in Egypt in 1899 and later moved to Jerusalem, was typical of those post-1880 Arab arrivals). It is estimated that as many as 500,000 Arabs arrived in Palestine between 1932 and 1944. The bulk of the Arabs living today in what was the territory of Palestine are descendants of people who emigrated from various Arab countries to take advantage of the economic opportunities that became available once the land of Palestine began to flourish at the end of the 19th century with the arrival of the Zionists. Those Arabs who arrived in Palestine in the 20th century did not have deep roots, or any roots, in the part of Palestine that became Israel (in the absence of precise census or land records, it is not possible to know with certainty the number of Arab Palestinians who had lived in villages and worked the land for centuries in the part of Palestine that became Israel).

Be all of that as it may be, I reiterate that I am acknowledging that the Palestinian Arabs, like the Jews, have a legitimate claim to the land in question. When two parties have rightful claims to an object or land or whatever, the conflicting claims can be resolved, and in the instant case a peaceful outcome can be reached, based on an honorable compromise involving both sides to the dispute. Peace between Israel and the Palestinians can only come through compromise, not by denying Israel its historical roots by distorting history. Plain and simple, the rampant denial of Jewish history is a major aspect of the Palestinian Arabs' rationalization of their rejection of Israel's legitimacy and right to exist and of their unwillingness to compromise by sharing any part of the land of Palestine with a Jewish state. If, on the other hand, one agrees that the Jews are indigenous to the Holy Land, it follows that the establishment of modern Israel was justifiable and just, with all the implications that conclusion carries for the right of the Jews to possess at least a portion of the territory of Palestine.

CHAPTER 11:

Using Logic to Establish a Way Forward

So, where do I want to take this discussion now that I have voiced my agreement that the claim of an indigenous people (the Jews) to the land must be reconciled with what I will refer to as the "later" claim of the Palestinian Arabs to the same ground? Well, first, I need to repeat that the conflicting claims must be resolved through compromise. I cannot imagine any direction in which to proceed other than to seek an honorable compromise to obtain a peaceful outcome that will endure. But the real obstacle to resolving the conflict, namely the refusal of the Palestinian Arabs to accept the legitimacy and existence of Israel, has resulted in a lack of interest or willingness on the part of the Palestinians to reach a compromise. The Jews have always been willing to share the territory of what was Palestine with the Arabs, but the Palestinians are not now and have never been willing to share any portion of that land with the Jews. Since each group is making an essentially identical claim, i.e., each believes it has a right to own and occupy the same land, the sensible, logical, intuitive way to resolve the dispute is to work out a compromise, which in this instance would mean a separate state for the two peoples. That is what the 1947 UN partition plan was aimed at accomplishing. But no matter what grounds the Jews submit in support of their position that they are entitled to some portion of the land of Palestine, the Palestinians continue to covet the land all for themselves. Thus they persist in rejecting the legitimacy and right to exist of the modern State of Israel. So when I speak in this book of the need for compromise, I am referring to the compelling need for the two parties to agree to share the land of Palestine. The Palestinians have yet to recognize the concept of "sharing the land" as fundamental to resolving the conflict between the two sides.

Where am I heading with all this talk about compromise? Well, the Palestinians to date have refused to yield any meaningful ground regarding their unwillingness to accept the legitimacy and existence of Israel. And it is way premature to anticipate that any effort to prove that Israel's establishment was justifiable and just will bear any fruit. So, I thought I should attempt to apply some logic which might invigorate the reader's perspective, even if the introduction of logic into the equation won't jar the mindset of the Palestinians. (Remember that my goal is to impact those people who read this book who might be able to influence the Palestinians or be in a position to sway people who can influence the Palestinians – as implied in this book's Prologue, I have no delusions or illusions that I can directly influence the Palestinians with anything I say here.) I will proceed to fuse logic with the concept of compromise in just a moment, but initially I need to lay out the pertinent maxims of logic. Trying to bring logic into play is not meant as an abandonment of the position, about which no serious historian or archeologist can have even the slightest doubt, that the Jewish people are indigenous to the land of Palestine. But what the application of logic often does is validate the reasoning behind a conclusion, such as that the establishment of the modern State of Israel was justifiable and just.

So let's apply logic to the question of whether the land that became the modern State of Israel could have ever been the homeland solely of the Palestinians. Of course, it is where Arabs have lived since the fourth decade of the 7th century, where Jews have lived continuously for longer than the Arabs, and where approximately 540,000 Jews, as opposed to approximately 400,000 Arabs, lived in November 1947 when the UN partition plan was unveiled. Logic, drawing from these facts, tells us that Palestine was no less the homeland of Jews than of Arabs, and no less the homeland of Arabs than of Jews. So, logic dictates that the land that became Israel had been the homeland of Palestinians and Jews, not solely of Palestinians, and not solely of Jews.

And let's apply logic to the question of whether the land that became the State of Israel in 1948 could ever have been a land that belonged solely to the Arabs. It wasn't land that could have belonged to the Arabs at any point before the fourth decade of the 7th century when the Muslim Arabs first arrived in the Holy Land and conquered the territory of Palestine. Prior to the Arab conquest, Jews resided there. Following the Arab conquest, it was a region where both Arabs and Jews lived and have continued to reside. Logic, drawing from these facts, tells us that the parcels of land occupied by Arabs were Arab-owned land, and the parcels of land occupied by Jews were Jewish-owned land. So, logic dictates that the fact that Jews have continually owned plots of property on which they lived does not mean that the territory as a whole ever belonged only to the Jews any more than Arabs having owned parcels of property on which Arabs lived means that the territory as a whole ever belonged exclusively to the Arabs.

Here is where logic and the idea of compromise become entwined. If logic dictates that the land of Palestine had been the homeland of both the Jews and Palestinians, and that the mere ownership by Arabs and Jews of parcels of land in Palestine means that the territory of Palestine never belonged solely to either the Jews or Palestinians, then the Palestinians stood to lose nothing they already possessed if they had agreed to a compromise that involved dividing/sharing the contested region. Remember that the idea of partitioning the land of Palestine had initially been proposed by the Peel Commission in 1937, and then by the UN in 1947 when the international community came to a consensus that the fairest way to resolve the conflict was through the creation of two states – one Jewish, the other Arab. One can't consider fairness in a vacuum. So, in adopting the partition approach, the international community no doubt weighed such factors as (a) the violence by Arabs against Jews in Palestine during the 1920's and 1930's indicating that the Arabs could not live peaceably beside Jews, (b) the perception that the claims of the two sides were irreconcilable and the conflict could only be resolved through a compromise involving a partitioning of the land, (c) the connection of the Jews with their ancestral homeland, (d) the right of the Jewish people to a homeland in Palestine as embedded in international law, and (e) that even the Balfour Declaration did not recognize a right exclusive to the Jewish people to all of the territory of Palestine – the British document in support of the creation of a "Jewish national home" in Palestine was conditioned upon nothing being done to prejudice the "civil and religious rights" of the non-Jewish communities in the territory. But no matter what reasons applied to the finding of fairness, the fact is that a partition plan, i.e., a plan to share the contested territory, was approved by the UN based on the consensus of the international community that it was the fairest method to apply to resolve the conflict. The words "fairness" and "fairest" are the operative words here. Why?

Again, I need to emphasize that the Palestinians would have lost nothing by agreeing to a compromise based on a partition plan given the logical considerations cited above. That compromise would not have come at the expense of the Arabs in general or the Palestinians in particular. It would not have taken or stolen anything from the Arabs, resulted in the displacement of Palestinians, or otherwise caused them a "loss." Rather, and most decisively, it would have formally recognized what had been the reality ever since the Muslim Arab conquest of Palestine in the 7th century, specifically, that the land had served as the homeland of both peoples and never belonged solely to the

Arabs or the Jews. If no "loss" was suffered by the Palestinian Arabs when the State of Israel was established in 1948, then there is no valid argument to be made that the partitioning of the region then known as Palestine was unfair, and thus no basis for the continuing opposition of the Palestinian Arabs to Israel's presence in the Middle East. In other words, if the creation of modern Israel did not result in a "loss" to the Palestinians, then you can reasonably conclude that the establishment of Israel in 1948 was fair, and thus justifiable and just.

Unfortunately, the Palestinians have never attempted or been inclined to view the situation from the standpoint of fairness. That is because if they regarded the partitioning/sharing of the land of Palestine as fair, they would be acknowledging Israel's legitimacy and right to exist in the Middle East. I am familiar with the phrase that what is fair is in the eye of the beholder, so I can see why one might argue that if the Palestinians did not believe the UN partition plan was fair, then it was not fair. Of course, that sort of thinking disregards the alternative line of thinking to the effect that the Palestinian rejection of the UN partition plan was based on the Palestinians' feelings, and that feelings can ignore reality and basic truths. With respect to the Palestinian objection to the UN partition plan, I submit that the plan was fair because its implementation would not have caused any "loss" to the Palestinians, and the creation of Israel according to the plan would therefore have been justifiable and just.

I, of course, anticipate that the logic I have applied, which dictates that the land of Palestine is both a Jewish and Arab land, will serve to validate the reasoning adopted by those readers who have concluded or are leaning towards concluding that the creation of Israel in 1948 was justifiable and just. I am also hopeful that even Palestinians who reject the Jewish people's powerful claim to at least some portion of the land of Palestine can be convinced to reconsider their refusal to accept the legitimacy and existence of Israel. After all, the logic applied above does not draw from or rest upon the historical connections of the Jews to the land of Palestine that the Palestinians continue working so hard to debunk. We all are aware that when the UN voted in 1947 to create two states by partitioning Palestine, the Jews accepted the proposal, but the Arab countries categorically and violently rejected the UN partition plan. As history has recorded, peace is no closer today than it was in 1947. Peace would have blossomed in 1947 had the Palestinians (and the Arab world in general) accepted the UN partition plan. This plan granted to both peoples, to the Jews who were a majority in the land allocated by the plan to the Jewish state and to the Arabs who were a majority in the land given by the plan to the Arab state, the right of self-determination. It is not too late for the Palestinians to agree to an honorable compromise. What they now need to do is acknowledge with relative unanimity that the State of Israel is legitimate and has the right to exist where it was born in 1948 (the Palestinians having presumably first been convinced that the establishment of Israel was justifiable and just), and to then enter into good faith negotiations with Israel to resolve outstanding issues.

Behold! I see the pathway to an enduring peace if the Palestinians reverse course. The Palestinians must not allow time to slip away. Conventional wisdom always held that time was on the Palestinians' side, that the Arab world would "get its act together" and that Israel would become isolated as the world became frustrated with Israel's failure to make peace happen. But things have not been trending in that direction. Time appears to be working in Israel's favor. The Palestinians need to unequivocally recognize the legitimacy and right to exist of the State of Israel and promptly get themselves to the negotiating table. Just returning to the negotiating table without first abandoning their rejection of Israel's legitimacy and existence likely will not do the trick. Foremost, then, is the imperative that the Palestinians be convinced that Israel's creation was justifiable and just, which in turn will clear the way to them accepting Israel's legitimacy and right to exist.

CHAPTER 12:

The Palestinian Point of View - Is It Credible?

As we have seen, the Arab world rejected the Balfour Declaration from the moment it was issued in 1917, opposed the partition plan approved by the UN in November 1947, which the Zionists and their movement accepted, and invaded Israel in May 1948 aiming to destroy the nascent state. Notwithstanding whatever is contained in the Palestinian narrative, the truth is that the Palestinians have rejected for over one hundred years the right of the Jewish people to a sovereign state anywhere in the Middle East, even in some tiny portion of that locale. The Palestinians annually celebrate the Nakba, marking the "tragedy" of the Palestinians, namely the failed invasion of Israel and the birth of the modern State of Israel (the Arabic word "Nakba" refers to any catastrophe inflicted on a blameless people by an overpowering force, in the instant situation that force being the Zionists). Nakba day is celebrated on May 15, the day after David Ben-Gurion proclaimed Israel's independence, clearly evidencing that the Palestinians perceive that the catastrophe that befell them was Israel's creation and survival. In simple terms, the Palestinians refuse to accept Israel's legitimacy and the right of the Jewish state to exist.

I have described several opportunities to obtain their own state that the Palestinians have squandered, and of course, there are many other examples such as Israel's offers in 2000 and 2008 of a state that would have included Gaza, the West Bank (subject to some land swaps), and East Jerusalem. History and events have proven that the Palestinian "cause" has been, and remains, far more focused on their goal of destroying Israel than it is on obtaining their own state. Jews long ago became reconciled to sharing the Holy Land with Arabs. But where is the call of Palestinians to recognize Israel's sovereignty over at least some portion of its ancestral homeland? No such call has been forthcoming because the Palestinians aren't convinced that Israel's establishment was justifiable and just. By accepting the validity of the historical links of the Jews to the Holy Land, and by accepting that the Jews are indigenous to the territory of Palestine, the Palestinians would hopefully be propelled to recognize the legitimacy and right to exist of the Jewish state. I am again reminded of the huge shift in position that I am urging the Palestinians to adopt.

Given the ongoing denial by the Palestinians of the primary historical truths that confirm the ancient Jewish presence in Palestine, a pattern of denial that is tied to their refusal to accept Israel's legitimacy and right to exist, the reader might wonder whether my head is screwed on correctly when I now suggest that it is essential to try to gain an understanding of the point of view of the Palestinian people, as opposed to that of the Palestinian leadership which largely echoes the mistruths set out in the Palestinian narrative. Is there something to be learned from members of the Palestinian community that could explain some basis for Palestinians wanting to end Israel's presence in the Middle East other than the falsehoods drawn from the Palestinian narrative that are hurled by Palestinian and other Arab leaders at anyone who will listen? Is there an emotional side to the Palestinian point of view to take into account and which might lend weight to the rationale of those who reject Israel's legitimacy and right to exist? I have heard so often in my life the caveat that I should avoid being judgmental about a viewpoint based on someone's personal experience unless I also had the same experience. I guess I am referring to the axiom that one should not criticize another's viewpoint without first walking in that person's shoes. Well, I must concede that I have never walked in the shoes of any Palestinian, and that the most effective approach to learning what the Palestinian people think, while at the same time abiding by that axiom, would be for me to conduct personal interviews of Palestinians to obtain their side of the conflict in their own words. But that task would have been more of a challenge than I was willing to accept, due not only to time constraints imposed by my schedule and the considerable expense such a project would have caused me to incur, but also because I could not have predicted that those whom I decided to interview would express themselves in a manner that would be helpful to my purpose. So I have opted to present a quote that I found in my readings that I believe is comprehensive in scope and contains the most heartfelt expression of the Palestinian perspective that I have come upon.

The quote that I have selected appears in Israeli journalist Ari Shavit's book about Israel, "My Promised Land." The quoted language, attributed to a Palestinian-Israeli attorney with whom Shavit was conversing while they traveled together in Israel in 2003, reads as follows:

> There is no balance between my right and your right. At the outset, the Jews had no legal, historical, or religious right to the land. The only right they had was the right born of persecution, but that right cannot justify taking 78 percent of a land that is not theirs. It cannot justify the fact that the guests went on to become the masters. At the end of the day, the ones with the superior right to the land are the natives, not the immigrants – the ones who have lived here for hundreds of years and have become part of the land just as the land has become a part of them. We are not like you. We are not strangers or wanderers or emigrants. For centuries we have lived upon this land and we multiplied. No one can uproot us. No one can separate us from the land. Not even you.

At another point in the same conversation, the attorney told Shavit, and I am using Shavit's words here, that the Palestinian catastrophe of 1948 was not exactly like the Holocaust, but that he (the attorney) was not willing to accept the Jewish monopoly on the term "Holocaust." Shavit then quotes the attorney as follows:

It is true that here, there were no concentration camps. But on the other hand, unlike the Holocaust, the Palestinian catastrophe of 1948 is still going on. And while the Holocaust was the holocaust of man, the Palestinian catastrophe of 1948 was a holocaust of man and land. The destruction of our people was also the destruction of our homeland.

It is clear from Shavit's commentary associated with the above-quoted language that the attorney's remark that "the Palestinian catastrophe of 1948 is still going on" refers to the attorney's belief that Israel has failed to solve the problems caused by the presence of the Arabs who never left Israel in 1947-48 or who returned to Israel after the War of Independence (as some did), and that Israel has never addressed the Palestinian refugee problem. Shavit also notes that the attorney does not believe that the Israelis are willing to give Palestinians their elementary rights, leaving the Palestinians with no alternative but to continue what Shavit refers to as the "struggle."

As for any comments from me about the above quotes from the Palestinian-Israeli attorney, I prefer not to engage in a sparring match with those unable to counter, in print in this book, the many criticisms I am tempted to offer of his expressions of deep indignation over the fate of the Palestinians as a consequence of the Jews gaining a state of their own. (I will note that I am annoyed by his reference to the Jews "taking" 78 percent of the land – the controlling consideration needs to be that the 1947 UN partition plan gave roughly 55 percent of the land to the proposed Jewish state, and to the extent the 55 percent subsequently rose, which it did, that increase occurred solely because of victory achieved by Israel in its War of Independence, a war of aggression initiated by the Arabs against Israel after it attained statehood). I believe I have previously addressed much of the content of the attorney's quoted remarks at various points in this book. What strikes me, in particular, is that none of the attorney's statements offer any rebuke to the position of the Palestinian leaders, both past and present, that the Jewish people have no right to a national home in the land of Palestine, that the Jewish State of Israel has no right to exist in the Middle East, and that all of Palestine belongs to the Arabs. I appreciate that the attorney's words are passionate and deserving of attention if for no other reason than that anyone who grieves over a claimed injustice should not be ignored. However, I doubt, even if words similar to the attorney's mournful description of events had been communicated in the form of a warning to leaders of the international community before that community acted to support the Zionist movement's goal of obtaining a Jewish homeland in Palestine, that the level of support that was offered would have diminished. I will leave it to the reader to judge if the historical, archeological, and other forms of evidence I have presented are sufficient to outweigh the attorney's emotional plea, which of course completely ignores, among other key points and elements, the continuous 3,000 year connection of the Jewish people to the Holy Land and the fact that the Jewish people are indigenous to the land of Palestine.

I want to take a moment to review. At a certain point in time, the Palestinian Arabs began to resent the influx of Zionists into

Palestine. Jews, for the reasons previously discussed, believed they had the right to emigrate to Palestine. The 1947 UN partition plan affirmed that right. However, the Arab world, including the Palestinians, took the position that the UN did not have the prerogative to grant a portion of the land of Palestine to the Jews, not even a portion where a majority of the population was Jewish. So, within hours of the moment when the State of Israel was proclaimed on May 14, 1948, the armies of five Arab countries, together with Palestinian paramilitary forces and volunteers from other Arab states, attacked Israel with the distinct aim of destroying the new state. That war was started because the Arab world, including the Palestinians, insisted the Jews had no right to be present in Palestine and that the State of Israel was illegitimate and had no right to exist. Israel's War of Independence ended with the drawing of cease-fire lines. However, the Palestinians' war against Israel continues to this day since they still believe the Jews do not have the right to be present in the Holy Land, and that Israel is illegitimate and has no right to exist. On the other hand, Israel has every intention of remaining in existence. I know of no country that is inclined to yield to efforts to terminate its existence. No one should underestimate Israel's will to remain a feature of the Middle East map. I am reminded of a story involving former Israeli Prime Minister Golda Meir. She is reputed to have said that if the Jews had not battled the invading Arab armies and were annihilated in 1948, the Jewish dead would have received beautiful eulogies worldwide. Instead, they stood their ground, but as the winners, they received condemnation from much of the world. According to the story, Meir commented that she would take the condemnation over the eulogies.

I need to briefly address several other arguments that have been advanced that reflect a Palestinian point of view. First is the oft-heard assertion that the Jews are "foreigners" to the land of Palestine, their only link to the land being a religious bond. Well, let's keep in mind that the great bulk of the Palestinians (or their descendants) who lived in Palestine when Israel declared its birth as a nation had arrived in Palestine after the Zionists began reclaiming the land and creating economic prosperity starting in the late 1890's. So, isn't it correct to conclude that if the Jews were "foreigners," so were the Palestinians? Then there is the argument that establishing a Jewish state in the Middle East created a threat to the continued existence of the Arab Palestinians. The only retort I can muster to that claim is that if you find it raises a compelling concern, then you would probably be captivated by a charge that Israel poses a threat to the continued existence of the world's elephant population. Next, there is the argument that the land that became Israel was historically under the rule of Arabs. Such a sentiment badly distorts history. Arabs had no connection to Palestine until the Muslim conquest in the fourth decade of the 7th century. The Christian Crusaders captured Jerusalem in 1099 and reigned until 1187. Arabs then ruled again until 1249, but never after that. From 1517 to 1917, the land of Palestine was ruled by the Ottoman Empire, i.e., by the Turks, who are not Arabs. The fact of Arab rule, as just noted, hardly qualifies the land that became Israel as having been "historically" under the rule of Arabs. And finally, I'll bite my tongue and refrain from blasting those who argue that the creation of Israel according to the UN partition plan would have resulted in the Palestinians being deprived of their right to self-determination. The Palestinians would have had their own state if they had accepted the UN partition plan. Consequently they would have been free to seek whatever level of gratification they desired due to their obtaining the right to self-determination.

There is a specific Islamic tenet that needs to be mentioned that ties into the Palestinian perspective and is a formidable impediment to the Palestinians abandoning their rejection of Israel's legitimacy and existence. I am referring to the principle in Islamic law that any land, once it has been ruled as an Islamic state, and whether or not the land was conquered by Muslims through the use of force, can never be allowed to revert to non-Muslim rule. Such land is deemed a waqf, or land dedicated as a religious trust in perpetuity. Muslims in general, including the Palestinians, believe that the land of Palestine is waqf land, and thus can never in the future be subjected to rule by any non-Muslims. So in effect, the Palestinians are committed to the struggle not only to liberate the land that is now Israel but also are fighting on behalf of Islam. Let's assume one accepts the premise, as promoted earlier in this book, that Israel's creation was founded on the basis of international law. In that case, it is difficult to comprehend what place a religious principle has in determining the outcome of the Israel-Palestinian conflict.

As I have stressed throughout this book, I believe that the only path to peace between the two sides is if the Palestinians finally accept with relative unanimity the legitimacy and right to exist of the State of Israel. It is time for the Palestinians to stop denying the fact of the enduring presence of the Jews in the Holy Land for some 3,000 years. It is time for the Palestinian leadership to put an absolute and permanent halt to the multiple efforts, in which they engage and which they orchestrate, to indoctrinate the Palestinian people into believing that the facts proving the connection of the Jewish people to the land of Palestine are concocted. It is time for Palestinians to stop responding with acts of terror to the existence of Israel. If the Palestinians want their desire for nationhood to be respected, to achieve their oft-announced goal of establishing a Palestinian state, and truly want lasting peace with Israel, they must accept the legitimacy and existence of the State of Israel, no ifs, ands, or buts. Once they do so, and assuming acts of terror and violence against Israel's Jews come to a halt, I believe with all my heart the great majority of Israeli Jews will fall in line with, and support, Palestinian aspirations for a widely-respected nationhood and the establishment of a Palestinian state. Remember, Israel is a democracy, one with flaws but a democracy nonetheless. In any democracy, the leaders of the government are accountable to the will of the people. Those leaders, even those of an Israeli government about which you may have questions or doubts concerning its policies related to the peace process, are subject to the electorate's demands. Call me naïve, or a fool, or silly if you wish, but I am willing to bet that if a majority of Israelis recognize that the Palestinians have genuinely accepted Israel's legitimacy and right to exist, a true and enduring negotiated peace between the two peoples not only becomes a possibility, but quite likely. The alternative outcome is that peace will remain a vain hope. Hopefully, the evidence I have presented supports the argument that Israel's establishment was justifiable and just and will "grease the wheels" that need to be spun to end, once and for all, the rejection by the Palestinians of Israel's legitimacy and existence.

I am aware that a few Arab countries (Egypt and Jordan, with the United Arab Emirates, Bahrain, and Morocco falling in line in late 2020), as well as the Palestinian Authority, have to one extent or another recognized the fact that Israel exists, which must be distinguished from a recognition of Israel's right to exist. Based on events in late 2020, progress is being made by Israel and the Arab world in the normalization process. Still, one must distinguish between the integration of Israel into the community of Middle East nations and acceptance by the Palestinians of Israel's presence, legitimacy, and right to exist. Perhaps the wider recognition of Israel by Arab states may eventually prompt the Palestinians to come to the negotiating table in a reoriented frame of mind. But I believe it is fair and accurate to say that many Israeli Jews aren't convinced that the Palestinians have abandoned the goal of destroying Israel. Until that goal is relinquished, and that will occur only when the Palestinians accept with relative unanimity the legitimacy and existence of the State of Israel, it makes logical sense to proceed in this discussion on the basis that the Palestinians do not accept Israel's legitimacy or support the country's right to exist.

My assertion that there are solid grounds for the Israelis to remain suspicious of Palestinian intentions regarding Israel's survival should not be viewed as hyperbole. When Hamas took control of Gaza, the great majority of the Arab residents of the West Bank supported Hamas also coming to power in the West Bank notwithstanding that Hamas had clearly and widely declared its goal of destroying Israel. Also, I find survey data released in 2020 particularly instructive and compelling. One poll reported that 66 percent of Palestinians residing in the West Bank and 56 percent of Gaza residents pick "regaining all of historical Palestine for the Palestinians, from the Jordan River to the Mediterranean Sea" as the top Palestinian national priority during the next five years. Another poll found that 64 percent of Palestinians favor a return to armed struggle in response to the U.S. peace plan put forward in January 2020. Such poll results strongly suggest that the Palestinians do not accept Israel's legitimacy and right to exist and that they want to see Israel destroyed or otherwise conclusively uprooted.

CHAPTER 13:

The Impact of Anti-Semitism

It is probably accurate to assert that any discussion of anti-Semitism, which is often referred to as the world's oldest social disease or the world's oldest hatred, is little better than useless. Why I believe that to be so will be discussed in some detail below, but at the heart of the seemingly futile confrontation with the world's anti-Semites is the apparent impossibility of logically dealing with something irrational. And let me inject at the start of this chapter that perhaps the term anti-Semitism, which was introduced in 1879 by a German Jew-hater who called for the murder and banishment of Jews, should be revised to "Jew-hatred" since the acts and speech that target Jews are anti-Jewish, and the people who hate Jews are Jew-haters. When Arabs are slandered due to their ethnicity, no one refers to that phenomenon as anti-Semitism, even though the act or speech is directed at people who are also Semites. But this book will stick with the term anti-Semitism because that is the phrase commonly used to describe behavior that reflects a hatred of Jews.

And I want to clarify at the outset that I do not pretend to have any answers to the knotty issue of anti-Semitism. So if you are looking for proposed solutions to the problem, please seek them elsewhere. Nor is this chapter's purpose to attempt to determine the fundamental cause(s) of anti-Semitism. It is to point to the rationale for why the widespread existence of anti-Semitism throughout the world further supports the argument that Israel's creation was justifiable and just.

Some pertinent background about anti-Semitism will hopefully shed light on the justifiability and justness of Israel's establishment. It is well-documented that Christian anti-Semitism in the form of intense persecution of the Jews, fed by Christian theology and attitudes, began in earnest with the advent of the Crusades in the 11th century. Scholars and others have written and pontificated on the subject of anti-Semitism ever since. They've studied the problem to a fare-thee-well, yet still, the true root of anti-Semitism has never been deduced from a lengthy list of purported causes. That list includes, for example, and in no particular order:

a) hatred of the Jews (mostly by Christians) due to the belief in the slur that Jews killed Jesus;

b) objection of non-Jews to the unwillingness of some Jews to leave behind the culture of the country from which they came;

c) irritation felt by non-Jews to the sluggish pace at which Jews may adapt to the prevailing culture (Germany's

Jews attempted on a large scale to integrate themselves into German society for several decades before the 1930's, and look what happened to them);

d) the view that Jews are culturally or otherwise inferior (especially when the country's dominant culture categorizes Jews as immigrants);

e) the dislike of Jews because they are culturally or just simply different from others, an impression reinforced because Jews often live in separate communities (I'd note that people often live in neighborhoods composed of people like themselves and I'd ask whether Jews may have developed that habit because for centuries they were forced to live in ghettos, and even in America could not live in whatever community they may have desired to buy a home?);

f) the envy and jealousy caused by the accomplishments of Jews in science, the arts, business, entertainment, etc.;

g) the resentment felt by non-Jews that Jews are guilty of dual loyalty;

h) contempt on the part of non-Jews as a reaction to their perception that Jews who do not assimilate exhibit a sense of superiority;

i) the exasperation of non-Jews prompted merely because the Jews, as a scattered minority, are not willing to be absorbed by the majority;

j) the supposition that Jews are wealthy (which raises the curious question of why there has never been any sustained persecution in world history against wealthy non-Jews, and also ignores the well-proven history that both poor Jews and rich Jews have been equally despised);

k) ill will toward Jews due to the perception that they control the banks and the media;

l) the envy felt by non-Jews as the result of the economic achievements of many Jews (could it be that such accomplishments are a result of Jews being left with no choice over the centuries but to become self-reliant?);

m) Jews are detested by non-Jews because the Jewish people consider themselves God's "chosen people" (notwithstanding that Christians and Muslims claim to be chosen people under the theology of their faiths, but those who practice Christianity and Islam have never been condemned for claiming to have been "chosen");

n) the acceptance of the outlandish charge that Jews control the world; or

o) the belief in the conspiracy theory that Jews collaborate to spread evil across the globe or that there is a secret international group of Jews that controls the world economy (it is bewildering that Jews can be deemed inferior, yet capable of dominating the world's economy or even the whole world).

And believe me, I can extend this list considerably. In any event, to the best of my knowledge and understanding, no one has yet offered a universally accepted reason that unambiguously explains what generates expressions and acts of anti-Semitism.

I hasten to emphasize an essential distinction between the demonization suffered by Jews and the vilification of African-Americans, Muslims, and others. Only the Jews are the subject of bigotry that accuses them of controlling governments, countries, world events, and this, that, and everything else, and of deviously plotting to take over the world (or of having already succeeded in doing so). In the eyes of the anti-Semites, only Jews pull all the strings.

Note that I have not, and will not, attempt to sort out the type of anti-Semitism that flows from the left side of the political spectrum as opposed to what oozes from the political right or to distinguish between that which is spewed by the radical left or radical right or by radical Islamists. That is because it does not matter, certainly for purposes of this chapter, from which political direction the foul winds blow. I have listed some likely causes of anti-Semitism solely to serve as a reminder that there is virtually no end to the explanations or to the list itself. Those who hate Jews will never have a problem unearthing a rationale or implausible explanation for their anti-Semitism, be it related to how Jews look, pray, or live, or to some virulent conspiracy theory that places the blame on the Jews for the problems the world faces.

It is certainly more true than not that historically anti-Semitism has increased when a society or country faces unrest due to insecurity. It is a natural human instinct to search for some-one to blame when a society's stability is threatened. In such a setting, the Jews are likely to be blamed for the changes or threatened changes, especially if no solid evidence surfaces to provide a logical explanation for why a situation has developed that has caused societal trauma. The most obvious example of this sort of scapegoating is what happened to the Jews in Germany in the years following Hitler's rise to power. But nothing erases or alters the reality that there has not been a time during the past one thousand years of Jewish history in which vicious anti-Semitism of one ugly degree or another did not fester, and not solely to demean Jews, but also with the broader goal of eradicating Judaism.

Anti-Semitism has never been, and is not today, confined to any one particular class of people or groups of countries. It is certainly not limited to people of any specific intellectual level. Nor is any country immune to anti-Semitism. Even in countries where one can count the number of Jews on one hand, Jews are nonetheless the subject of anti-Semitism. No better illustration of that is Malaysia, a country with hardly any Jewish citizens, where the man who has served for several recent years as Prime Minister (he resigned from that post in February 2020, following his ruling coalition's collapse) openly flaunts his anti-Semitism and is unrepentant and unashamed to do so. He has even declared that he is proud to be an anti-Semite.

Anti-Semitism in Europe

Let's look at anti-Semitism in Europe, and then we will turn to the situation in the United States. Anti-Semitism has long been entrenched in Europe, predating the Holocaust by roughly a millennium. It was in Europe that the blood libel evolved that Jews use the blood of Christian children to make Passover matzoh. That blood libel persists to this day. When the bubonic plague swept through Europe in the 14th century, the Jews were widely charged with responsibility. Thousands of innocent Jews were slaughtered after Jews were accused of poisoning wells to take revenge on Christians for suffering imposed on Jews. For centuries Jews were confined to ghettos across Europe. They were restricted to a limited number of professions, one being money lending, which generated the portrayal of Jews as ruthless profiteers. There was the violent emotional hatred that pervaded Czarist Russia and neighboring countries, and which produced "The Protocols of the Elders of Zion." This scurrilous publication trumpeted that Jews are the source of all evil by virtue of their scheming at secret meetings to control the world through war and economic strategies. Even today it remains the cornerstone for nonsensical explanations by anti-Semites for global unrest. The so-called Dreyfus affair in France, involving false charges of treason being leveled against a Jewish French army officer, is still familiar today. There was the Holocaust (for my present purposes, no more need be said on that subject).

Today, our world is challenged by a resurgence of anti-Semitism that is severely impacting Europe, where physical threats, violence, and murders have escalated in cities from London to Paris to Berlin. A 2019 survey conducted by the Anti-Defamation League reveals that a quarter of Europeans hold strong anti-Semitic views. Don't get me wrong. Europe today is not the Germany of the 1940's, or even of the 1930's, but the present groundswell of anti-Semitism isn't pretty. Anti-Semitic acts in France increased by 70% over a one-year period between 2017 and 2018 and by another 27% in 2019. The Netherlands documented a record number of anti-Semitic incidents in 2019. Anti-Semitism soared to a record high level in Great Britain in 2019. Commencing in 2015, the ranks of Britain's Labour Party became contaminated with anti-Semitism, and today that political party is battling the infestation. And 75 years after the Holocaust, verbal and physical abuse of Jews is reemerging on the streets and social media in Germany, where many people had assumed anti-Semitism had become a relic of the past. That was a faulty assumption if ever there was one. Anti-Semitic crimes in Germany in 2019 reached their highest level since the country started keeping such statistics, rising 13 percent over the 2018 level. The number of anti-Semitic incidents in 2019 in Austria was more than double that of five years earlier. Even in the Czech Republic, where anti-Semitism remains low compared with other European countries, anti-Semitic incidents occurred twice as often in 2019 as in 2018.

Four people were murdered in the Jewish Museum in Brussels several years ago, and acts of violence against Jews are an almost daily occurrence throughout Europe. Recent parades in Belgium and Spain have featured anti-Semitic images, including participants dressed in Nazi SS uniforms and as concentration camp prisoners. Orthodox Jews are depicted sitting on top of floats surrounded by money bags and with insect bodies. The results of a recent survey of Jews in Europe found that more than one-third considered emigrating in the five years preceding the survey because they did not feel safe as Jews in the European country where they live. Three-quarters of those surveyed said anti-Semitism has worsened since 2008. According to another recent survey, 20% of people polled in sixteen European countries believe that a secret network of Jews is influencing the world's political and economic affairs.

Anti-Semitism in the U.S.

The explosion in the number of anti-Semitic incidents occurring in recent years in Europe has been rivaled by what has been transpiring in the United States. According to the Anti-Defamation League, 2,107 anti-Semitic incidents were recorded in the U.S. in 2019 (including 61 physical assaults, 1,127 cases of harassment, and 919 acts of vandalism). This marks the highest annual tally since the organization began tracking anti-Semitic incidents in 1979, and represents a 12 percent increase over the number of incidents counted in 2018. The number of hate organizations operating in the U.S. is striking. According to the FBI, the victims of the majority of religiously motivated hate crimes in the U.S. every year since 1995 are Jews. Today, Jewish schools and places of worship in the U.S. are targeted. Armed security guards, metal detectors, and physical fortifications are now widely adopted security measures at Jewish institutions. Repeated anti-Semitic incidents of harassment, vandalism, and assault on college campuses create a hostile environment for Jewish students. Hate crimes committed against ultra-Orthodox Jews have become commonplace in the New York City area. Gravestones in Jewish cemeteries are desecrated with regularity, as are the walls of synagogues.

There is a surging white nationalist movement in this country. It was not long ago (2017) that white supremacists and their compatriots marched in Charlottesville, Virginia, rhythmically chanting "Jews shall not replace us." Eleven Jews were slaughtered by a white supremacist gunman in a Pittsburgh synagogue in October 2018. During the rampage, the shooter shouted "all Jews must die." In April 2019, a shooting at a synagogue near San Diego killed one worshipper. And in December 2019, three people were murdered in a kosher grocery store in Jersey City, New Jersey. Jews have long been the subject of accusations of spreading deadly diseases such as AIDS. So, it comes as no surprise that hatred against Jews is continuously sprouting on social media in connection with the coronavirus pandemic. It's rife with anti-Semitic conspiracy theories in which Jews are charged with, among other foul deeds, using positions of power to spread the virus. Someone will surely blame the Jews for the severe economic downturn precipitated by the pandemic. In America, as in Europe, the amount of anti-Semitic hate speech online has reached epidemic levels.

Let's not forget that the United States, like Europe, has a history of anti-Semitism stretching back generations. Does it come to mind that during the 1930's, thirty million Americans would listen to Father Charles Coughlin as he denounced the Jews on the radio? Do you remember the German-American Bund rally on behalf of the Nazi cause in February 1939 before a capacity crowd of more than 20,000 people at Madison Square Garden in New York City, with the arena pockmarked with swastikas? Do you recall that the U.S. during World War II refused to allow shiploads of hopeful Jewish refugees fleeing Nazi tyranny to obtain temporary refuge on our shores? Does the infamous Neo-Nazi march in Skokie, Illinois, in 1977 ring a bell? Then there have been the anti-Semitic rants of the Ku Klux Klan over the decades, and the rise (and subsequent dismemberment) of the American Nazi Party. And the charges that the Jews were behind 9/11, that it was an inside job carried out by Jews, still reverberate.

There is no doubt that many American Jews are somewhat comforted by the knowledge that in America, most non-Jews typically view any attack on Jews as unacceptable and will speak out against any such vile acts. Jews tend to believe that somehow America is different, that our government and our neighbors will not stand still for such behavior. But let's not sugar coat the seeming good fortune of Jews in America insofar as they have to date avoided the sweeping tide of anti-Semitism that has historically engulfed both Eastern and Western Europe in the form of exclusion, religious persecution, second-class status, and wholesale massacre. Today, there is a resurgence of anti-Semitism in the U.S., and the possibility has begun to emerge that maybe America is not different.

A major survey of American Jews disclosed in results released in the fall of 2019 that 88% of Jews in this country believe anti-Semitism is presently a problem, and 84% responded that it has become worse over the past five years. American Jews ignore at their peril the possibility that the perceived barriers to anti-Semitism becoming pervasive in America could quickly crumble and vanish due to presently unanticipated, but imaginable, events. I earlier said that the Holocaust would not be a subject of discussion in this book, and I have no intention of now delving into the Nazi regime's plan to systematically commit mass murder of all European Jews or any other facet of the Holocaust to refresh or enrich the reader's knowledge of those horrors. But I do want to underscore the point that the happenings and consequences of the Holocaust hold deep and critical lessons for our own time. Such cruelty and barbarity could happen here!

Anti-Semitism Aimed at Israel

Anti-Zionism is a form of anti-Semitism that has raised its ugly head in recent times. Whereas anti-Semitism was formerly directed against Jews as strangers in the lands of their residence, it now also targets Jews in their own land. Intolerance toward Jews is now aimed not just at Jewish people, but at the Jewish State of Israel. But you would be wrong to assume that there is any connection between the birth of modern Israel in 1948 and anti-Semitism directed towards Israeli Jews. As noted by former Soviet refusenik Natan Sharansky, "The Jewish state is no more the cause of anti-Semitism today than the absence of a Jewish state was its cause a century ago."

There was the famous "Zionism is racism" resolution passed by the United Nations General Assembly in 1975, which declared that Zionism is a form of racism and racial discrimination (there are many who refer to the United Nations as the world's cesspool of anti-Semitism given its institutional hostility towards Israel, but that is a topic for others to debate). That UN resolution was repealed in 1991. More recently, anti-Zionism has morphed into a vehicle for demonizing and striving to eliminate the State of Israel. Today's enemies of Israel will often protest that they are simply anti-Zionist, not anti-Semitic, notwithstanding that their words and actions threaten Israel's right to exist.

Please do not misconstrue my words. One can legitimately criticize the policies of the State of Israel without being anti-Semitic. Such criticism is often fair and principled, on top of which Israel itself has always been one of the world's most self-critical countries. Just read the daily press in Israel, or listen to debates in the Knesset. But the line between legitimate criticism of Israel and anti-Semitism is crossed when anti-Zionism demonizes Israel so that the message conveyed challenges Israel's continued existence. When anti-Zionism targets the right of Jews to statehood in Israel, it adopts the mantra of Jew-hatred under a new guise. It becomes anti-Semitism. And those who may not personally dislike Jews but support efforts to delegitimize Israel are complicit in the anti-Semitism. The U.S. State Department in 2010 adopted a definition of anti-Semitism that states in clear and unequivocal terms that anti-Zionism is anti-Semitism.

Muslim Anti-Semitism

No discussion of anti-Semitism today can avoid touching on anti-Semitism emanating from the Muslim world. It is a subject that runs the risk of further polarizing the debate, but the matter of a portion of the Muslim world being wrapped up in profound hate of Jews cannot be ignored as a significant factor in the Palestinians' rejection of Israel's legitimacy and right to exist. It is beyond reasonable dispute that the Arab leaders' strategy, and of the Arab world in general, including the Palestinians, has always been to prevent, and since 1948 to eliminate, the existence of any Jewish state in what is now Israel. In the words of the 1937 Peel Commission report, "The hatred of the Arab politician for the Jewish national home has never been concealed and . . . it has now permeated the Arab population as a whole." Although efforts to contaminate the minds of the world's Muslims with hatred toward Jews and Israel may not have produced consistent success, there can be no doubt that millions of Muslims are today inspired to incorporate Jew-hatred into their thinking.

I am no expert on Islam, but I am aware that the Koran runs the gamut, from declaring that Muslims must kill Jews to verses urging tolerance towards Jews and that the words of the Koran and the meaning of those words can be spun and twisted to suit the political aims of the spinner or twister. Among the spin masters are Muslims who hate the Jewish people for having the audacity to assert their right to a sovereign state in their ancestral homeland. But my aim here is not to try in any way to push for Muslim society and its clerics to examine or scrutinize the Koran to eliminate the ability of anti-Semites to draw religious legitimacy from the words of that document in support of their Jew-hatred. (However, it would be a terrific development if that sort of project was undertaken and completed, and positive outcomes implemented.) Instead, I am attempting to point out that hatred of Jews among Muslim Arabs, including among the Palestinians, is a major driver of the rejection by Palestinians of Israel's legitimacy and right to exist.

Notwithstanding that anti-Semitism has been a long-standing vehicle for expressing hatred of Jews, it is only within the past one hundred years or so that anti-Semitism has spread throughout countries where Muslims reside, to the point where it is almost as though anti-Semitism has become grafted onto the attitude about Jews that is expressed by so many Muslims. The issue cannot and must not be swept under the rug. Make no mistake about it, an anti-Jewish feeling among Muslims flourished long before the establishment of modern Israel. Jews living in Muslim countries were, before the 20th century, somewhat tolerated compared to Jews who lived in Christian lands, where intolerance, exclusion, and demonization of Jews were rife. However, Jews in Arab lands held the inferior status of dhimmi, which subjected them to restrictions in their daily life (but did allow freedom of worship).

But eventually, anti-Semitism migrated from the West and spread throughout the Muslim world, buttressed by anti-Semitic statements contained in several verses in the Koran. Anti-Semitism among Muslims was then reinforced in the 1930's when the Grand Mufti of Jerusalem (previously mentioned), a powerful member of the world's Islamic hierarchy who had been appointed to the post by the British government in 1921 and who bore an intense hostility toward Jews, began to make common cause with Nazi Germany regarding the genocidal ambitions of the Nazis. The Grand Mufti became a trusted Nazi ally, spending multiple years during World War II in Berlin, from where he delivered a daily pro-Nazi broadcast to the Muslim world. Following on the heels of World War II came the defeat by Israel of the Arab armies that invaded the new state in May 1948, and the subsequent destruction of Arab military forces and Israel's occupation of Arab land as a result of the "six-day war" in 1967, all of which further inflamed anti-Semitism in the Muslim world, a world whose culture is repulsed by shame. Then there is the jealousy and humiliation of Muslims over Israel's breathtaking success as a modern country that has still further stoked Muslim anti-Semitism.

Not only has vilification of Jews by Palestinians continued unabated for roughly the past 100 years, but one cannot ignore the reality, a chilling reality in my view, that the fundamentalists within Islam have evolved into a movement that holds the words of the Koran as the sole guide to religious truth. Therefore, insist the fundamentalists, Muslims must live by the strict letter of those words, i.e., must accept a literal interpretation of Islam, even concerning those verses that promote intolerance or hatred for other religious faiths or practices. I am sure that millions of Muslims do not hate Jews, and it is clear to me that millions of other Muslims do not even reveal any signs of anti-Jewish hostility. However, there are 1.8 billion Muslims in the world. The gist of the matter is that so many Muslims in terms of absolute numbers — we're talking about multiples of multiple millions — provide traction for the tenets of Islam that are drawn upon by proponents of radical Islam to justify hatred of Jews. Those multitudes of Muslims furnish that traction by not vigorously repudiating promptly and in unison, or otherwise speaking out in any meaningful way, in response to words constituting Jew-hatred spoken by the radical Islamists, fundamentalists, jihadists, extremists, arch-Islamists, or whatever you want to call them. Unfortunately, many Muslims who do not embrace Jew-hatred remain silent to avoid malicious criticism and threats of violence, and even violent acts of vengeance, from fellow Muslims.

I do not want to be viewed as trying to "tar" believers in a particular religious faith with a broad brush based on the actions of fringe elements within that religion. After all, virtually every religion, including Judaism, has its extremists, whose abhorrent beliefs should never be used to tarnish noble religious pursuits. But the issue here, and it must be recognized as posing a threat to the Jewish people, is that with their silence, those millions upon millions of Muslims who fail to denounce the hateful rhetoric of the radical Islamists become part of the problem by in effect sanctioning or even encouraging the words and actions of the haters. On the other hand, significant numbers of Jews will typically speak out strongly and forcefully against radical Jews who promote intolerance and/or hate of any other religion. Anger, frustration, disappointment, and even bitterness due to acts of violence and terror are all feelings expressed by Israelis about individual Palestinians. And situations have regrettably been uncovered where a rogue group of Jews involved in fomenting violence against Palestinian Arabs has adopted a hateful attitude towards the Arab community. But the Jews of Israel do not collectively encourage or sanction the injection of the poison of hate by Jewish extremists whose aim is to demonize the Arabs as a people.

On a similar note, I would be less than candid if I did not acknowledge that there have been instances, which from my standpoint have thankfully been relatively infrequent, of Israeli Jews committing hate crimes against Arab Palestinians. But the Israelis do not, and never have,. glorified or celebrated such actions, as do Palestinians when hateful crimes are perpetrated against Jews. The Israel government is quick to condemn hateful acts committed by any of its Jewish citizens. Bad actors face criminal prosecution and punishment in line with Israeli criminal law.

It is no coincidence that the Muslim world today is almost entirely free of Jews, some 850,000 Jews having been driven from

Muslim lands following the founding of Israel. And it is well-understood that Muslims living in Europe are far more anti-Semitic than the general European population. Anti-Semitism within European Muslim communities is reflected in almost daily reports of physical violence perpetrated by Muslims upon Jews throughout Europe. Muslims have committed the great majority of anti-Semitic acts involving violent physical attacks over the past twenty years in Europe. Several surveys documented that the percentage of Muslims in European countries that harbor anti-Semitic viewpoints is far more than the percent of the total population other than Muslims who hold such views. Now that Muslims represent a not-insignificant portion of the entire European population, and the percentage of Muslims is growing as the Muslim migration to Europe continues, the world has become increasingly aware of the impact that the Muslim presence has had on European Jewry. In a few European countries, such as Denmark and Sweden, anti-Semitism was unknown a hundred years ago. But today, given the increase in their Muslim population, the record of anti-Semitic incidents in those countries parallels the statistics in other European nations.

The anti-Semitism within Muslim society has become constant, with examples of expressions of anti-Jewish attitudes having become legion. Imams and Arab politicians rant to the Palestinian populace that the Jews stole their land, that the Palestinian people are victims of the evil and all-powerful Jews. The Palestinians are told that the Jews are the cause of all modern evils, Jews have been the enemies of Islam since the 7th century, Jews must be wiped out because they are the major symbol of the

Western world and its civilization, Jews are behind the project to enslave humanity, the Jewish threat to humanity can be halted only by exterminating all Jews, the Holocaust never happened, Israeli soldiers indiscriminately and maliciously target Palestinian children, Jews are plotting to defile Islamic holy places situated on the Temple Mount (such false allegations tend to provoke violence against Israeli Jews), and on and on it goes. The sad truth is that I have only skimmed the surface in citing unfounded toxic Muslim sentiments reflecting rage against Jews. I should note that these sorts of anti-Semitic denunciations prove the worthlessness of the argument that Muslims hate the Zionists, not people of the Jewish faith.

One cannot overstate how Muslim hatred of Jews flourishes today among many Palestinian Muslim Arabs. Muslims name streets, schools, and sports teams after murderers of Jews. Anti-Semitic Muslims view deadly attacks on Jews not as a violation of Islam, but as a pathway to martyrdom. Terrorists are incentivized to murder and maim Jews by cash payments to Palestinians convicted of attacks against Israeli Jews and the families of terrorists killed during such attacks. We all have heard the reports of Muslim clerics extolling incitement against Jews, and on occasion calling for the death of Jews. Palestinian children are raised to glorify and exalt any Arab who kills a Jew, so consequently, suicide bombers and other sorts of terrorists are looked upon as role models. Palestinian youth are brainwashed to aspire to martyrdom by carrying out terror attacks against Jews. They are being taught in school to hate Jews and Israel through a blend of anti-Semitic rhetoric and radical Islamic concepts. It is a sign of utter disdain for Jews and Israel that the nation of Israel does not appear on maps of the Middle East published by the Palestine Authority. At international sports events, Arab athletes typically are still unwilling to extend an Israeli opponent the courtesy of a handshake.

And I could fill many more pages with examples of incitement against Jews that are communicated through Palestinian media channels. The official media of most Arab states, and of the Palestinian Authority, continues to this day to incite violence and hate against Jews based on their religion and to hurl venom at the existence of the Jewish state itself. The problem of Muslim anti-Semitism is confounded by the circumstance that, as was the case with the press in Nazi Germany, the mainstream press in Middle Eastern countries is controlled by the regimes that govern the Muslim people. This results in the unfortunate consequence that anti-Semitism becomes embedded in the minds of the readership and disproving the vitriol becomes a virtual impossibility. And I will but mention in passing the threat to Jews emanating from an ideology that is spreading in many quarters that justifies Muslim anti-Semitism as an expression of legitimate political grievance.

In an earlier chapter dealing with Palestinian refugees, I raised a rhetorical question about what one is to make of all the Arab violence against Jews in Palestine that occurred long before the Palestinian refugee problem arose in 1948. In the context of the refugee problem, that question did not require any further consideration because, at that juncture of the book, I was not searching for an explanation for the pre-1948 Arab violence against Jews in Palestine. However, in the context of the instant discussion about the hate of Jews felt by many Muslims, that question needs to be addressed. History establishes that Arab violence against Jews in Palestine pre-1948 was unrelated to the plight of Palestinian refugees, or, for that matter, to Israel's occupation of the West Bank or the presence of Jewish settlements in the West Bank, since none of those circumstances existed before 1948. All of the violence and terror against Jews in Palestine that occurred between 1920 and May 14, 1948, much of which was described previously, took place prior to the establishment of the State of Israel. If the State of Israel did not yet exist, if Israel's birth had not yet been proclaimed, how can one not rationally conclude that the pre-1948 violence against Jews was a result of Jew-hatred? What else besides Jew-hatred can explain the killings and violence by Arabs during the 1920's and 1930's when the Jews in Palestine had not yet obtained either the political power to impose what might be perceived as oppressive measures upon the Arabs or the military prowess or capability to gain possession of land other than through legal acquisition?

As much as I would like to include an appeal to the Palestinians to abandon the path of hatred for Jews, I know that any such plea from me would be futile because I do not have the wisdom to offer a prescription for how a people might combat their hatred for other people. What I am hoping, perhaps irrationally (but grasping for straws in connection with Muslim hate for Jews is about all I see as an option), is that the hate will begin to dissipate once the momentum of a sincere effort to reach a lasting peace has taken hold. We can anticipate that that momentum will build once the Palestinians are convinced that Israel's establishment was justifiable and just, thereby providing the Palestinians with the impetus to forsake their position that Israel is illegitimate and has no right to exist.

It is time for Palestinians to stop hating the Jews and Israel and to end their perpetual war against Israel. It is time for the Palestinians to renounce their courses of action and reaction based on Jew-hatred, to accept Israel's legitimacy and right to exist, and to seek a negotiated resolution to the Israel-Palestinian conflict. What has happened in the one territory (Gaza) where Palestinians have gained self-rule does not offer cause for optimism. Gaza's leaders and citizens remain consumed by hatred of Israel and Jews. But we must persist in the battle to convince the Palestinians that Israel's establishment was justifiable and just so they can then explain to the world why they have shifted from a position of rejection to one of acceptance of Israel's legitimacy and right to exist. There does not appear to be any other approach, at least in the foreseeable future, that offers the promise of producing an end to the Israel-Palestinian conflict. Meanwhile, the all-consuming hatred of Jews and of Israel with which the minds of so many Palestinians are obsessed continues to prove calamitous for the Palestinian people in terms of political and social decline.

Anti-Semitism brings into play the challenge to Jews, especially those Jews imbued with Judaism's spiritual traditions, of effectively countering the hatred inherent in anti-Semitism. But the task becomes even more daunting when one considers the findings of a 2014 global survey of anti-Semitic attitudes conducted by the Anti-Defamation League across 102 countries. The survey found that 77% of respondents who hated Jews had never before met a Jew. If that finding doesn't help explain why hatred of Jews knows no boundaries, then nothing can or will.

No one should be astonished to learn that some do not believe that any formula or process will ever be uncovered that can be successfully employed even to deter, let alone bring to a halt, the depraved rants of the anti-Semites. After all, the most focused and concerted effort ever undertaken to find a cure for the sickness of anti-Semitism, namely seventy-five years of post-Holocaust education and anti-racist legislation, has been of little if any avail. Apparently, it will not be practical or possible to negotiate, legislate, or educate anti-Semitism out of existence, nor has any amount of verbal confrontation of anti-Semites or the increased prosecution of hate crimes made an identifiable dent in the problem. Although I fully support efforts to combat anti-Semitism in every conceivable manner, and we must never abandon the fight, it seems as though the pull-out-all-the-stops strategies that have been implemented have fallen far, far short of the mark. I am not normally prone to surrender to perpetual gloom, but it can certainly be surmised that anti-Semitism will not disappear or be minimized any time soon.

So why, you might be asking or wondering, have I bothered to touch on what is, by any set of criteria, nothing more than a smattering of history and the more recent impact of anti-Semitism? Why is it that I have not merely left you to find your path to becoming better educated about anti-Semitism? My reason for explaining the phenomenon of anti-Semitism as I have done in this chapter is that, as alluded to earlier, I believe it is a forceful foundational element in support of the argument that Israel's creation was justifiable and just. Just as Palestine came to be regarded as a refuge for the Jewish people, so too is the continuing presence of the State of Israel a critical consideration if Jews in the Diaspora should at any moment in the future feel compelled by circumstances to escape from the oppression of anti-Semitism. This opportunity to seek refuge from anti-Semitism must be available to all Jews, even those who may be indifferent to Judaism's spiritual aspects. The last one thousand years of history have proven beyond a shadow of a doubt that the Jewish people require an easily accessible place where they can obtain refuge should the scourge of anti-Semitism anywhere in the world rise to a threatening level, however Jews may choose to define the term "threatening level." Israel is that place.

History is filled with instances where Jews have been assured they were accepted as citizens of a particular country, only to discover later that they were no longer welcome and were forced to flee and find a home in another country. Israel's existence, secured by that nation's ability to defend itself, represents the best guarantee that never again will the Jews have to wait futilely for others to defend or save Jews in peril. Given what I have had to say about the repulsive force of anti-Semitism, both in the past and in the world today, doesn't the awareness that there is an accessible haven for Jews from this sort of oppression count for something significant and justify in and of itself the justifiability and justness of the establishment of Israel? You are encouraged, even urged, to consider this rationale for why Israel's creation was justifiable and just as part of the total package of considerations to be weighed, keeping in mind that my ultimate goal is for the Palestinians to accept Israel's legitimacy and right to exist after first convincing them that the establishment of Israel was justifiable and just.

CHAPTER 14:

Conclusion

Well, there you have it. The "it" you now have is one person's take on what must happen to establish the foundation for a lasting peace between Israel and the Palestinians. The Palestinians must be convinced that the establishment of the modern State of Israel was justifiable and just, which in turn will open the door to the Palestinians abandoning their long-standing rejection of Israel's legitimacy and right to exist. If that door opens, the real obstacle to resolving the Israel-Palestinian conflict will be crushed. The Palestinians will no longer be intent upon rejecting the concept of negotiating an enduring peace with Israel because they will no longer entertain their hope of destroying the Jewish state. I am confident that once the Palestinians accept the Jewish people's right to their own nation, solutions to the contentious issues that will need to be ironed out to produce an enduring peace agreement will be both formulated and agreed upon.

As I have previously commented, Israel is not about to disappear from the map of the Middle East. Israel is here to stay. Even some of Israel's most strident enemies now recognize that Israel has become too economically and militarily powerful to destroy. The Palestinians need to accept the reality that Jews are no longer willing to return to the days when they were a wandering people and when they struggled century after century to survive as a scattered minority. Jews have no reason to believe that their plight under such circumstances would be any less oppressive in the future than it was in the past.

Yet the Palestinians remain unyielding in their refusal to accept the legitimacy and right to exist of the Jewish State of Israel in the Middle East. They have had numerous opportunities to secure their own state. Still, they have always refused the chance to end their stateless condition because they have been more determined to attempt to eliminate the Jewish state than to obtain their own country. Their leaders have wasted those opportunities while pursuing an agenda that has included inciting violence and hate against the Jews and Israel, glorifying murderers of Israelis as martyrs, manufacturing shallow excuses for why they have rejected negotiating a solution to the impasse between the two parties, formulating their version of history in an attempt to erase the ancient connection of the Jews to their ancestral land, and blaming Israel for the absence of peace in the Middle East. They have neglected to make time to initiate substantive efforts to construct the institutions of statehood (other than to build a Palestinian police force), and of course, they have never come to terms with the idea of ending their resistance to Israel's continued existence. The Palestinians have not shown any ability or intention over the past hundred years to forsake their efforts to prevent Jews from having a state in the Middle East, even within a tiny portion of that region.

The Arab world, including the Palestinians, has been obsessed with the Jewish state since its creation, expending vast sums on weapons to be used in wars fought against Israel and financing its anti-Israel propaganda machine. Rather than pursue their opportunities to resolve the Israel-Palestinian conflict, the Palestinians have followed the Arab countries' lead in rejecting all peace overtures no matter the source. Following the "six-day war" in 1967, Israel offered to negotiate peace with the Arabs and to return land captured during that war. But representatives of eight Arab nations met in Khartoum, Sudan, and issued the famous Khartoum Resolution in which they announced what became known as the "three no's" – the Arabs would not recognize Israel, negotiate with Israel, or make peace with Israel. When the Israel-Egypt peace accord took effect on March 26, 1979, most of the Arab world reacted with outrage. Egypt, which at the time was generally considered the leader of the Arab world, was expelled from the Arab League after the peace treaty was signed (the Arab League had been formed in 1945 in part to oppose the formation and presence in the Middle East of a Jewish state). These are but two of virtually countless notable examples of past expressions of Arab world unwillingness to accept a Jewish state in the Middle East and welcome Israel as a member of the community of nations.

The Jewish presence in the land of Palestine over the eighteen centuries commencing in 70 C.E. through to the late 1800's may have been relatively small in terms of absolute numbers, but it was, as emphasized throughout this book, a continuous presence. It was that constant historical connection of the Jewish people with the land of Palestine that accounts for Israel's international legitimacy because that roughly 3,000 year link of the Jews with their ancestral homeland convinced the principal international organizations to support the creation of a Jewish state. It is my opinion that no one with any sense of objectivity can deny that some portion of the land at issue qualifies as the homeland of the ancestors of today's Jews. But, as I have repeatedly stated, much of the Arab world, the Palestinians in particular, cannot and will not accept the legitimacy and right to exist of the modern State of Israel, as small in size as that nation may be. Rather, Arab governments, leaders, media, and clerics, including those who speak to or on behalf of the Palestinians, continue to encourage anti-Jewish and anti-Israel attitudes among the Arab populace. Instead of showering the Palestinian people with talk about coexistence and peace, they talk about conflict and struggle. Instead of accepting Israel's legitimacy and right to exist, they expend their energy scheming Israel's demise. Instead of striving to build their society, they work to destroy Israel. Most people seek to learn and benefit from their neighbors, but the Arab world has made Israel a target of venomous hate. Regrettably, the Palestinians have been encouraged to stick to their intransigent position not only by the leaders and governments of Arab states, but also by Turkey and Iran. Perhaps there is a "bright side" to the recent development that it has fallen to Turkey and Iran, both non-Arab nations, to push the Palestinian cause. It is suggestive of the closer relationships, many occurring behind the scenes, that are developing between Israel and several Arab countries.

So what are my expectations? I am not looking for the Palestinians to admit that they have been wrong in rejecting the legitimacy and right to exist of the State of Israel, or that they are responsible for the failure to arrive at a peaceful solution. I am not anticipating or expecting that the Palestinians will concede that if they had accepted the UN partition plan, there would have been no war with the Jews following the plan's approval by the world body, and thus no Palestinian refugee problem. I am not requesting the Palestinians to cast criticism upon the poor choices made and decisions reached by their leaders over the decades. Neither am I demanding that the Palestinians extend any apologies for the acts of terror committed against Jews and the hateful and hurtful words hurled at Jews and about Israel over past decades. Nor am I expecting the Palestinians to unveil a startling new vision of peace. I do not insist that the Palestinians praise the Zionists who found the will to rebuild a sovereign nation in their ancestral homeland. I will understand if the Palestinians do not express remorse for perpetuating the conflict between the two sides by turning virtually every action taken by the Israeli government regarding Palestinians into a grievance. I am not interested in hearing the Palestinians acknowledge that they made a grave mistake in favoring violence over a compromise that would have seen the Palestinians agree to share the land of Palestine with a Jewish state. I have no interest in forcing the Arab world to publicly face up to its own failings, or confess that the so-called Palestinian narrative is replete with distortions and mistruths.

All I want from the Palestinians is that they accept the legitimacy and right to exist in the Middle East of the State of Israel in a show of relative unanimity. I reiterate that there is no need for the Palestinians to admit mistakes or offer apologies. I am urging them to acknowledge that Israel's creation was legitimate and that it has the right to exist. It is, of course, the purpose of this book to help in the effort to convince the Palestinians that the establishment of the modern State of Israel was justifiable and just, which I anticipate will, in turn, prompt the Palestinians to accept Israel's legitimacy and its right to a permanent existence.

I've had enough of the incitement and violence and terror against the Israelis, of the sacrifice of Palestinian lives in a misdirected cause that is referred to by some as delusional, and of the relentless imposition by the Palestinians of unrealistic demands upon Israel. The Palestinians remain stateless. The conflict continues with no apparent end in sight. Certainly, if it turns out that the Palestinians are ultimately unwilling to make peace with Israel on any terms, then this book will have been for naught. If the Palestinians ultimately prove unable to dispense with their seeming all-or-nothing approach to the impasse, then this book will have served no purpose. If the world is to witness a new beginning to the end of the impasse, the Palestinians must take the bold step of coming to terms with what

I have argued is the real obstacle to resolving the Israel-Palestinian conflict. That obstacle, which by now is presumably indelibly impressed in your mind, is the continued rejection by the Palestinians of Israel's legitimacy and right to exist.

Speaking of boldness, we all understand that the best kind of peace between countries at loggerheads with each other is one derived through an agreement between negotiators determined to achieve peace. That means credible Palestinian leaders standing up and openly and willingly expressing recognition by the Palestinian people of Israel's legitimacy and the country's right to exist. I do not know that there are leaders among the Palestinian people, either presently or waiting in the wings, who today are strong enough politically and tough enough mentally to cool the passions of the Palestinian Arabs and endure the shock waves that will surely be produced by such an extreme reversal of stance. A key element will be for the leaders to persuade the Palestinian people that the act of compromise in the instant circumstances, i.e., agreeing to share the land of Palestine with the Jews, is not akin to treason. The Palestinian leaders who undertake that challenge must, of course, be prepared to persuade the Palestinian people that the Jews are truly indigenous to the land between the Jordan River and the Mediterranean Sea and that the continuous connection of the Jewish people with the land of Palestine for 3,000 years is not contrived.

We must remind ourselves that leaders have arisen throughout world history who were bold enough to make controversial moves to further the best interests of their people, knowing full well that the process of moving forward would require the movement's leadership to rally the populace to be accepting of heading in a new direction. We need Palestinian leaders who have the strength to accept past military defeats and losses of territory resulting from those defeats, and who have the foresight to want to build a prosperous future for their people, which starts by entering into a reconciliation process with the Israelis. I am confident, if not positive, that there are courageous Palestinians who can and will emerge in the near future who will rise to the occasion. And I am also confident that this generation of the Palestinian people, with the right leadership, will reveal their political maturity by opting to peacefully share the land of Palestine with the Jewish people. From my perspective, the Palestinian people will not have to swallow their pride in doing so because they will obtain in return, through good faith negotiations between both sides, a long-sought-after sovereign state of their own.

My most fervent wish contains three components:

1. The Palestinians accept reality with respect to clearing the path to peace with Israel.

2. The Palestinian people come to the realization that their focus needs to be on building a better future for themselves.

3. The Palestinians declare themselves ready to make peace with Israel by accepting that nation's legitimacy

and its right to a permanent existence in the Middle East, thereby removing from the picture what I believe is the real obstacle to peace.

Throughout this book, I have tried to provide the reader with relevant facts and logic that will enable you to thoughtfully and intelligently decide whether Israel's establishment was justifiable and just. You have read the arguments in support of that position, namely that:

1. The right of the Jews to a homeland in Palestine was recognized and ratified by the international community.

2. The right of the Jews to a homeland in Palestine was embedded in international law.

3. There is a continuous historical linkage of the Jews with Palestine.

4. Archeological findings prove the historical link of the Jewish people with Palestine.

5. The Jews are indigenous to Palestine.

6. Israel's size is infinitesimal as a percentage of the land area possessed by the Arab world.

7. Israel offers an accessible haven for Jews imperiled by anti-Semitism.

I have also put in play a theory, based on logic, that the creation of modern Israel did not result in any "loss" to the Palestinians, so that the country's establishment in 1948 was fair, and thus justifiable and just. And I have also discussed the various allegations leveled by the Palestinians to rationalize their rejection of Israel's legitimacy and right to exist, and have argued that none of them undercut or distract from the proposition that Israel's establishment was justifiable and just. The choice of a valid viewpoint is in your hands.

If you agree with my view that Israel was justifiably and justly created, you are now positioned to press the point with whomever you choose that the conflict between the Palestinians and Israel can be resolved once the real obstacle to peace is eliminated. As I have attempted to demonstrate, the most likely means of successfully confronting and overcoming the rejection of Israel's legitimacy and right to exist is by convincing the Palestinians that the establishment of modern Israel was justifiable and just. Let us hope that the Palestinians will soon turn the corner. The future of Israel-Palestinian relations need not remain a captive of inevitable conflict.

ACKNOWLEDGMENTS

In June 2007, my wife, Leslie, and I traveled by train through the Canadian Rockies. Not long after the adventure began, we met Keith and Jan Perring, residents of Sydney, Australia. The four of us became virtually inseparable for the remainder of the trip. Within hours of our introduction, Keith offered his opinion that the Palestinians had been placed in an "unfair" situation due to the establishment of Israel in the land of Palestine in 1948. What began as a friendly chat about a controversial subject evolved into a ten-year email exchange in which Keith and I unhesitatingly expressed our views on all aspects of the Israel-Palestinian conflict. That decade-long exchange served as the foundation for this book. I am grateful for Keith's willingness to keep the dialogue going for all those years and for his respectful challenges to my opinions. By the way, Keith and I continue to be in touch by email. It remains to be seen whether my book will have the desired impact on Keith's perspective.

I also want to thank my son, Zach, who lived in Israel several years ago and has a solid grasp of the issues surrounding the conflict between Israel and the Palestinians. Thanks as well to Rick Berkman, my long-time tennis partner who often visits Israel and is very tuned-in to the implications of the conflict. Both Zach and Rick read the initial manuscript and made many thoughtful and constructive suggestions. I am also appreciative of the helpful advice I received from my sister, Julie Curson.

My deepest gratitude goes to my daughter, Eden, who served as my masterful editor. Eden magically turned some clumsy phrasing into more transparent prose. There was hardly a paragraph that went untouched by Eden's editing.

And to my wife, Leslie, I want to express my most profound appreciation for her helpful comments along the way. Leslie deserves extra commendation for having provided so much meaningful encouragement as I pieced my thoughts together and attempted to write them coherently.

I want to acknowledge that much of the timeline and other information set out in this book's initial chapter (about Zionism) was drawn from "My Promised Land" by Israeli journalist Ari Shavit. I also found helpful overall the writings of Israeli historian Benny Morris and American Jewish Committee CEO David Harris, and hundreds of blogs and articles authored by too many people to cite.